The
Billy
Mitchell
Story

ALSO BY BURKE DAVIS

Novels

Whisper My Name
The Ragged Ones
Yorktown
The Summer Land

Biography

They Called Him Stonewall
Gray Fox: R. E. Lee & The Civil War
Jeb Stuart, The Last Cavalier
Marine: The Life of General Chesty Puller, USMC
The Billy Mitchell Affair

History

To Appomattox: Nine April Days, 1865
Our Incredible Civil War
The Cowpens-Guilford Courthouse Campaign
The World of Currier & Ives (with Roy King)
A Williamsburg Galaxy
Get Yamamoto

For Young Readers

Roberta E. Lee
America's First Army
Appomattox: Closing Struggle of the Civil War
Rebel Raider, A Biography of Admiral Semmes
   (with Evangeline Davis)
Yorktown: The Winning of American Independence

The Billy Mitchell Story

BURKE DAVIS

CHILTON BOOK COMPANY
Philadelphia / New York / London

To Donnie Perry

Contents

DEATH KNELL
OF THE BATTLESHIP

In the glow of a July sunset in the year 1921 an aged DeHavilland biplane, a relic of World War I, circled at sea sixty-five miles east of the Virginia Capes. Her pilot leaned from the cockpit to inspect a huge ship anchored beneath him.

The pilot was Brigadier General William Mitchell, Air Service, U.S. Army, forty-two, a handsome, fearless prophet who was in the next two days to become one of the most renowned living Americans.

The ship below was battered and rusty, but she was painted with target circles of red, white and blue, visible from far away. She was the 27,000-ton German battleship *Ostfriesland,* a veteran of the battle of Jutland, where she had been hit by eighteen large shells and struck a mine, yet had made her way into port. She had four skins and many watertight compartments and was said to be an unsinkable ship.

Mitchell admired her: ". . . like a grim old bulldog

with the vicious scars of Jutland still on her . . . she was sullen and dark and we knew we had a tough nut to crack." Mitchell turned shoreward in the last light of day, homing toward a short sandy landing strip at Langley Field. Tomorrow he would lead the bombers of his little air force in the first assault from the skies against a battleship.

For weeks that summer his makeshift squadrons had hammered at lesser German vessels in these waters, joining Navy and Marine Corps bombers in the test of planes against surface ships. One by one the target ships had been sunk until now the tests had reached their climax—a submarine, a destroyer and a cruiser had been destroyed. The nation waited to see whether Mitchell could also sink a great modern battleship. Newspaper headlines had stirred public excitement to a fever pitch. As he flew home, the Assistant Chief of the Air Service knew that the first triumphs would be forgotten if his crews failed tomorrow: "the development of air power might be arrested. . . . We had to kill, lay out and bury this great ship."

An audience of military men from many nations had gathered for the show. Hundreds of dignitaries had spent the blustery night ashore, including General of the Army John J. Pershing; Secretaries Weeks, Denby and Wallace of Army, Navy and Agriculture; Assistant Secretary of Navy Theodore Roosevelt, Jr.; eight Senators and a dozen Congressmen; Admiral William Fullam, Commander Richard E. Byrd and Lieutenant Commander Zachary Lansdowne of the Navy; General John A. Lejeune of the Marine Corps; several Army chiefs, including Generals Charles Menoher of the Air Service, C.C. Williams of Ordnance and A.A. Fries of Chemical Warfare.

Glenn Martin, the young plane-builder, had come to see

his new bombers tested. A special guest of Secretary Denby was General Pietro Badoglio, with an Italian air mission. Other observers had come from England, Japan, France, Spain, Portugal and Brazil. The naval transport *Henderson* alone bore three hundred guests, about fifty of them newspaper reporters. During the night ashore at Old Point Comfort and on the ships of the Atlantic Fleet in Hampton Roads, the betting was heavily against Mitchell and his bomber pilots.

For six months Mitchell had been calling incessantly for these tests—though he had been preparing for them since he had returned from war early in 1919, preaching the gospel of air power as the decisive arm of the future, citing the lessons of the battle of St. Mihiel, in which he had commanded 1500 Allied planes, driven the Germans from the sky, and dominated the battlefield. He had been in headlines almost daily since his return from the war, but not until January, 1921, when he appeared before a Congressional committee headed by Representative Daniel Anthony of Kansas, had he staked his future, and that of air power, on a duel of planes against battleships.

He had confidently told the Congressmen that he could "destroy or sink any ship in existence." He sharply criticized an earlier test staged by the Navy, displaying charts and diagrams of air attack on an old warship, until Representative C. Bascom Slemp of Virginia, asked, "Why is it, if your statements are true—and I'm not casting any doubt upon them at all—that you aren't able to convince the high-ranking officers of the Army? Why can't they see the light?" Mitchell replied cautiously. He would later attack infantry officers who had never been off the ground, yet enforced regulations which stifled aviation—but to the Congressmen he said simply:

"We are presenting the situation to you, and we're ready to demonstrate this thing. If you allow no air force, not only will an opposing fleet land at will, but their aircraft will fly all over our country."

He fenced with the committee for hours until Slemp said wearily, "It seems to me that the principal problem is to demonstrate the certainty of your conclusions." It was just what Mitchell wanted to hear. "Give us the warships to attack," he said, "and come watch it." Within a few days resolutions in the House asked the Navy to turn over target ships to Mitchell and his bombers. Mitchell wrote to his engineering chief, Colonel Thurman Bane, at McCook Field, Illinois, "We are going to smoke these people out that do not believe in the air business and either make them fish or cut bait."

Soon afterward, when Senator William Borah of Idaho called for a halt to naval construction until Congress could plan "a modern navy," Secretary of Navy Josephus Daniels announced that the Navy would hold tests at sea, planes against battleships. The Air Service would be invited. Daniels made the front pages with his challenge: he was so confident that bombers could not hit a moving battleship that he would gladly stand on her deck while planes attacked. The public was fascinated by the vision of a personal duel between Mitchell and Daniels; this was the controversy reduced to its simplest terms. The public was anxious for the tests and was in no mood for ifs, ands or buts. The average American neither knew nor cared that pilots in the Navy were fighting as hard for aviation against their superiors as Mitchell was in the Army. The man in the street saw Mitchell as a gladiator, alone in his arena.

Mitchell wrote Colonel Bane to demand action. "I want

you to be sure to have what bombardment ships you have ready to be used with their crews when the attack of warships takes place. This to my mind is the most important thing we have before us."

Bane's shocked reply hinted that the engineer thought Mitchell had lost his mind. "Your letter . . . in which you say you want me to have bombardment ships ready for the attack on warships, is a little perturbing," he wrote. "Of course, you know we have no crews assigned to ships. In fact, we have not a single officer who ever dropped a bomb with a bombsight or ever was instructed to drop bombs with the idea of hitting a target."

Bane did not realize that such details meant nothing to Mitchell. The general was determined to make history off the Virginia Capes, and the lack of trained men, big planes, big bombs and all else were trifling obstacles. No warship had ever been sunk from the air. Bombsights were primitive. The largest American bomb weighed eleven hundred pounds, attack planes were untested, nearly all veteran bombardiers of the war were gone. No Army fliers had practiced in overwater navigation. Langley Field was a sleepy post with seven instructors and eight or nine students.

To Mitchell this was only a challenge. He stripped the Air Service of available pilots and planes at every post, from as far as Texas and Michigan, until he had about one thousand men and two hundred and fifty planes at the base under wartime secrecy. Crews were soon dropping bombs on the outline target of a battleship in the marshes near Langley Field—practice that drew complaint from Army headquarters: "Attention is called to your violation of Supply Circular No. 62 . . . in constructing one model battleship for target practice before funds are allotted."

Mitchell pushed on as if he realized that national security might be at stake. Practice continued.

He ordered giant bombs created almost overnight. One day he called in Captain C.H.M. Roberts of Ordnance. "Do we have a bomb that will sink a battleship?"

"No, we don't."

"Can you make one?"

"Yes, sir."

Mitchell glared at him as if he were wasting precious time. "There are a couple of details," Roberts said. "First, we've got no money." (The Ordnance budget of that day was about $100,000 a year.)

"How much do you need?"

"Half a million dollars."

"I'll have that for you tomorrow morning," Mitchell said.

Roberts was soon off to Frankford Arsenal. He and an associate sat up all night sketching bombs that weighed two thousand and four thousand pounds, big enough, they thought, to sink anything that floated. Ordnance officers, worried over Mitchell's furious pace, soon anxiously asked the Chief of Staff "to what extent it is intended to obligate funds for this purpose." A sharp reply came back. "The Secretary of War has not approved a program for such tests, and no obligation is authorized . . . until such a program is approved." Somehow—it is still not clear just how—Mitchell wangled the money, and the big bomb program proceeded full steam ahead.

Captain Roberts and a team of pioneer ordnance men turned out the huge bombs at Aberdeen Proving Ground, using seamless steel tubes of a type used for torpedoes. They designed a fool-proof detonation system running entirely through the bomb, which was to be packed with one thousand pounds of TNT—the cap of the detonator was an ordinary 12-gauge shotgun shell. The pouring of so much TNT involved new problems, for the melted explosive had to be poured in small batches, allowed to cool and crystallize, and imperfections bored out. The process was slow, and Mitchell had little time, so the big bombs were packed in ice and stood under batteries of electric fans while the stubborn explosive was cooled.

Mitchell uprooted young George Goddard, his photography specialist, from McCook Field. "I want you to handle the newsreel and movie people—all temperamental. I want newsreels of those sinking ships in every theater in the country, just as soon as we can get 'em there." Goddard gathered eighteen DeHavillands for his photographic planes and wheedled a small dirigible from Aberdeen to carry his newsreel crewmen.

Mitchell put radio specialists into an adjoining office in Washington's old Munitions Building and ordered them to plan a radio network to link his bombers with Langley Field and with portable radio stations along the coast. He assigned meteorologists to work with the radiomen.

The green crews at Langley quickly gained skill. Their hits on the battleship target were 50 per cent or less at first, but in May, the most veteran squadron, the 14th Heavy Bombardment, neared perfection.

Mitchell came down from Washington for a pep talk to the First Provisional Air Brigade, as he now called it. He reminded the men that they were on historic ground. Hampton was the oldest continually inhabited town in British America. Nearby, Cornwallis had surrendered, and General McClellan had dug in with Federal troops during the Civil War and had made use of the first military aircraft—the balloons of Professor Thaddeus Lowe. Through

waters offshore the first English settlers had come to James-
town, British and French fleets had fought in the Revolution, and the *Monitor* had overcome the *Merrimac*. He
spoke of resistance to progress which had become a military and naval tradition. The young men of the Air Service cheered him and went back to work.

The pilots were wary of some Mitchell innovations,
especially radio. They thought it only a toy, and found
headsets in their helmets uncomfortable. When they returned from flights to report malfunctions of the sets, they
were sent back aloft until they reported adequate recep-
tion.

A shortage of money plagued Mitchell. Colonel Bane's
budget was so limited that he could not send telegrams,
but was forced to write. Mitchell tried to bring his old
friend Hap Arnold from his post in California, but there
was no money for transportation. He asked permission to
have a row of tall pines cut at the edge of Langley, and
was refused—until two young men were killed when their
bomb-laden small plane struck the trees and exploded.

Near the end of training there was a crisis when Mitchell found that the new Martin bombers were unable to
carry the giant bombs.

Mitchell glumly reported, "The one Martin at Langley
can't make the motors turn up and apparently the ship
won't lift the load it is designed to lift." But there was a
sudden success. A daring test pilot, Lieutenant Carl Cover,
skimmed over the pines with a bomb load of 2512 pounds.
The Brigade was ready.

In final conference, Mitchell and the Navy agreed that
the tests would be held at sea off the Virginia Capes,
though it would mean round trips of two hundred miles
for Mitchell's planes, many of which had limited gas ca-

pacities. He warned the Navy that pilots must not be held up over the targets. The Navy replied that inspections of ships must be made after each bombing, so that effects of hits and near-misses could be seen. Without such controls, naval officers said, the tests would be meaningless. Mitchell's aim was much simpler—to convince the American people that planes could sink ships.

On June 20 Mitchell and his aide, Captain St. Clair (Wingbone) Streett, flew out in an old DeHavilland, the *Osprey*, a pampered ship with a new engine, her fuselage painted blue above and white below, fluttering a long blue command pennant at the tail. The first act of the spectacle was over quickly. The German submarine U-117, the smallest and most fragile of the targets, was bombed by the Navy with enthusiasm; she had sunk nine Allied ships during the war, many of them helpless fishing vessels off New England. Two waves of Navy F-5-L bombers broke the hull in two, and she disappeared. Mitchell wrote, "None except the air people had expected such a rapid termination. . . . These bombs tore her all to pieces. . . . Some of the skeptics began to be convinced. . . ." But the sub was not a heavy capital ship. The true tests were still to come.

Three weeks later the second target was attacked, the G-102, a long-range destroyer built just before the war, 312 feet long and thirty feet abeam. Mitchell's attack was led by eighteen pursuit planes in three flights, staggered so that they could meet enemy planes at any altitude. Next came the light bombers, De Havillands with 100-pounders, and last would come the heavy Martins, with 600-pound bombs. "It was the first time in aeronautical history," Mitchell said, "that an attack had been made in this way. Every element of a large force was there."

The fighters dived almost on the deck, dropping bombs at thirty-second intervals. Mitchell wrote, "The attack was beautiful to watch. . . . Practically every bomb went where it was directed. The decks of the destroyer were punctured and swept from end to end." He later waved in Captain W. R. Lawson and his heavy Martins for a quick kill. As Mitchell saw it, "In less time than it takes to tell, their bombs began churning the water around the destroyer. They hit close in front of it, behind it, opposite its side and directly in its center. Columns of water rose hundreds of feet into the air. For a few minutes the vessel looked as if it were on fire. Smoke came out of its funnels . . . it broke completely in two in the middle and sank out of sight. . . . All our methods and systems of bombing had proved to be correct."

Langley roared after dark, Mitchell recalled. "That night all our men had returned safely . . . after their first great experience in bombing. Their rejoicing was tremendous. They knew now that unless something most unusual happened it would be proved for all time that aircraft dominated seacraft."

Five days later the crews faced a more formidable target, the light cruiser *Frankfurt*, six years old, 5100 tons, shielded with side armor and buoyed by many compartments. Mitchell thought she was almost too beautiful to bomb. "As she lay in the water, she resembled a swan, so gracefully did she ride the waves. I hated to sink her, as she was far more attractive than any of the seacraft looking on." The *Frankfurt* withstood a rain of light bombs; goats and small animals caged on the decks were dead, but the ship was still sound below decks.

Lawson's big bombers appeared at 3:30 P.M. and struck

without waiting for another inspection. As Mitchell recorded the next moments:

"The bombs fell so fast that the attack could not be stopped before mortal damage had been done to the ship. The control vessel made the signal to cease as the good ship was toppling over . . . tremendous columns of water shot up . . . fell in tons on the deck of the ship, sweeping it clear . . . the cruiser . . . sank rapidly."

George Goddard's photographic planes had been working in relays, and as soon as movie film of the sinking reached Langley, Goddard flew off with it to Bolling Field, where newsreel men would meet him, hurry it to New York, and then to big-city theaters.

The Navy was still cheerful despite the cruiser's end. If a light ship could withstand such punishment, the *Ostfriesland* would be far tougher. Two days later, on July 20, the Atlantic fleet and its guests steamed out before dawn. A heavy sea was running under a northeast wind that gusted to thirty knots. The bombing schedule was postponed from hour to hour. At 1 P.M. when his bombers still had not been called, Mitchell flew out with Streett to investigate. They were stopped short of the target. "To our astonishment we saw the whole Atlantic Fleet making for the Chesapeake Bay. . . . We found that since there was about a twenty-knot wind blowing they determined an airplane could not act." Mitchell signaled that he wanted to begin bombing, and the fleet returned to the targets.

Until 3 o'clock Navy and Marine planes dropped small bombs on the battleship with little effect. The umpires were on the target when Captain Alfred Johnson, the Navy air commander for the tests, got a surprise message from shore—the Martin bombers had left Langley without orders and were coming to attack. The planes arrived, led by Lieutenant Clayton Bissell. Mitchell called Johnson on the control vessel, "Must attack in forty minutes. Fuel limited." He was told to send the bombers back if they were short of gas, but Mitchell refused and they circled until about 3:30, when they were allowed to begin with their six hundred-pound bombs. Bissell's men released five bombs in rapid succession, with two or more in the air at once, scoring hits on the deck and alongside, causing serious damage to the upper works. Mitchell said, "We felt the jolts and noise of the explosion in the air 3000 feet above." But it was the end of the day's work, and the *Ostfriesland* had survived. A storm was breaking, and the planes left hurriedly.

Some of the observers were seasick, and two of the dignitaries, Secretary Weeks and General Pershing, decided to spend the next day ashore at Old Point Comfort, since it looked as if the ship would not be sunk.

Mitchell and his crews were delayed on the flight home, flying broad circles to escape the storm. Mitchell landed in a muddy peanut field, and only with the aid of farm horses did he reach high ground and take off again. Mitchell landed at Langley with the help of an emergency lighting system, rows of flaming tin cans burning a gasoline-kerosene mixture—using wicks made of woollen puttees. Mitchell stayed up most of the night to welcome the storm-tossed planes. Captain Lawson, who was forced down near Norfolk, broke a wheel and returned by car, train and ferry to report at 1 A.M., Captain Roberts arrived in a dirigible at 5 A.M., but George Goddard did not appear until the next day.

Mitchell had flown 660 miles to and from the target during the day's attack on the battleship and was "terribly overstrained." He had been unable to eat a meal for five days, keeping an orderly running after him with cups of coffee. But his failure to sink the *Ostfriesland* seemed only to spur him on. As his sister Ruth wrote, "Bill was mad clear through. Next morning, he decided, it was going to be 'kill or die trying.' "

Dawn brought clear, mild weather, perfect for flying. Mitchell took off before 7 A.M. with a flight of Martins led by Bissell, to watch the first round, the dropping of 1100-pound bombs. Navy planes were scheduled to join this attack, but Mitchell radioed that Bissell's men were on the way and asked that they not be interfered with by naval planes. He sighted the target and the audience. At about two miles from the tethered battleship was an armada of ships, eight of them United States battleships, including the new *Pennsylvania* and the antique *Olympia*, Admiral Dewey's flagship at Manila Bay. With destroyers and auxiliaries they formed a great circle about the target.

The bombers passed Mitchell in review, the pilots dipping wings in salute and Mitchell wagging the *Osprey* in response. The bombers began just before 8:30, as soon as the control ship, the *Shawmut*, gave the all clear signal by rolling up a white canvas painted with a red cross. Bissell dropped the first 1100-pounder, a direct hit on the forecastle. The next few moments provoked a bitter wrangle. The *Shawmut* made frantic signals to halt Bissell's planes, first with its canvas, and then with emergency smoke signals from its stack. Bissell's men were too quick and dropped four bombs, two more of them hits, but then they were waved away. The pilots flew toward home "mad as hornets" when the Navy halted them after one pass, forcing them to jettison other bombs they carried. They dropped them at sea—much too near the picket destroyers, the Navy complained.

Captain Lawson led Mitchell's last attack with six Martins and two Handley Pages each carrying a 2000-pound bomb—the giants which were, as Captain Hap Arnold said, "in basic design the same we were to use against Germany and Japan in World War II." Mitchell was briefing the pilots when the Navy radioed him to begin his attack. Captain Johnson explained that there had been a change in regulations. The bombers could bring out no more than three of these big bombs. Mitchell reacted furiously. "This was the last straw. We had an agreement with the Navy in writing that we would be allowed to make at least two direct hits on deck with our heaviest bombs." He disregarded Johnson's instructions, and the flight left with a bomb on each plane, eight in all. His last order to the pilots was, "Try for near-misses," for Captain Roberts and a one-legged Russian war veteran, Alexander de Seversky, had convinced him that near-misses in the water were more deadly than direct hits. Lawson led them down the runway and turned seaward. Mitchell radioed the Navy, "Martin bomber and Handley Page formation with 2000-pound bombs have taken off. . . . In case of failure to secure two direct hits, subsequent attacks will be made until we have secured the two hits the Army is authorized to make." Johnson did not reply.

Mitchell and Streett flew over the capes. Visibility was fair, with a haze above the target, and they had brief trouble in locating the fleet. Just after noon the attack began. When the first big bomb fell, observers watched as if the whole year's work rode with it.

It was longer than Navy bombs, dropped as straight as an arrow, and blazed in the sunshine. On impact a heavy water hammer blow was felt against the hulls of the *Henderson* and many warships. Mitchell wrote, ". . . up came the spout of water, more than any geyser, more than any missile made by man had ever produced. Three thousand feet above we felt the rush of air as it 'bumped' the wings of our plane. Higher and higher mounted the great water. . . . The old bulldog winced at the shock. . . ." Mitchell and Streett exchanged triumphant shouts over the roar of the *Osprey's* engine.

The next bomb missed, but at 12:21 a direct hit tore a gaping hole in the forecastle. Five minutes later another near-miss lifted the ship and threw a heavy fall of water across the deck—"like a Niagara," one reporter wrote.

The fifth large bomb fell near the stern, burying the quarter deck in water. The bow of the ship rose, and she began to slip under by the stern. Eleven minutes after the first direct hit, the sixth bomb struck less than fifty feet aft. The ship turned turtle, and water gleamed among her barnacles. Observers with field glasses saw split seams and holes in her bottom. One reporter said, "She rolled there like some immense, round, helpless sea animal."

In the *Osprey* the excited Streett stood in his cockpit shouting, "She's gone!" Mitchell described the end, "In a minute more there was only the tip of her beak showing above the water. It looked as if her stern had touched the bottom of the sea as she stood there, straight up in a hundred fathoms of water, to bid a last farewell."

Aboard the *Henderson,* as one reporter wrote, "the chins of Navy officers . . . dropped. Their eyes seemed to be coming out of the ends of their marine glasses . . . seemed to be watching the end of an era which began when Rome crossed the high seas and smote Carthage." Some admirals sobbed openly. A solemn group stood by the rail—two admirals, Secretary of Navy Denby and General Menoher, the Air Service Chief, Mitchell's crusty superior. These men did not speak as the great rust-encrusted hulk took its final plunge. It was as if the little knot of onlookers were attending a funeral for one of their dearest friends.

As the *Ostfriesland* vanished, this group walked silently aft. Menoher said at last, "I guess maybe the Navy will get its airplane carriers."

Mitchell swooped low over the ship's grave, and as he later confessed, he had tears in his eyes. "We wanted to destroy her from the air; but when it was actually accomplished it was a very serious and awesome sight. . . . I watched her sink from a few feet above her. Then I flew my plane to the *Henderson,* where the people . . . were waving and cheering on the decks and in the rigging."

The *Osprey* zoomed so low over the transport that men aboard saw Mitchell's grin and salute as he turned shoreward. The Navy was not yet willing to mark battleships for oblivion, but one admiral, William A. Moffett, was positive and almost as far-sighted as Mitchell. "The lesson is that we must put planes on battleships and get aircraft carriers quickly. . . . We should have a minimum of eight carriers." Glenn Martin said, "No fleet afloat is safe if it loses control of the air. . . . The sinking of the *Ostfriesland* will be epoch-making."

General C.C. Williams of Army Ordnance offered the day's most quoted comment from the ship. "A bomb has been fired that will be heard around the world." One reporter talked with the two Japanese observers, H. Katsuda and G. Shibuta, who had kept cameras busy during the bombing. "There is much to learn here," Katsuda said. "Very great experiment, profoundly exciting. Our people will cheer your great Mitchell and, you may be sure, will study his experiments." He also spoke of a Japanese-American war. "Should there be such a war America would have to fight it a long way from home. . . . It would be gravely embarrassing to the American people if the ideas of your General Mitchell were more appreciated in Japan than in the United States. Gratitude is not one of the attributes of democracy."

Mitchell returned to Langley in triumph. He found every plane that could fly above the field to greet him. Cannon boomed below. Officers, mechanics and crewmen waved and shouted. A crude sign on a hangar recalled the *Ostfriesland* as she turned turtle and sank to her grave, "We don't sink battleships. We loop 'em."

The mob rushed the *Osprey,* pulled Mitchell from his cockpit, hoisted him to its shoulders and milled about with him. Mitchell laughed until his eyes streamed with tears. Men in the crowd reached to touch or slap him, and his words were drowned by a small band. Mitchell left the uproar behind him and went to his quarters. Bonfires burned all night, the band played on, and people danced around the fires. One of his aides, Lieutenant Farewell Bragg, described the brief speech Mitchell made that night: "Well, boys, I guess we showed 'em today!. . . . In the war to come, and you'll see it, God will be on the side of the heaviest air force. What we did to the *Frankfurt* and the *Ostfriesland* is what will happen to all warships in future wars. And don't you forget it. Keep your eye on the sky!" Mitchell watched the men celebrating from his window for a long time, saying fondly, "Darn those boys. But, by gosh, they did it!"

He hardly slept that night, watching the excited men. His sister Ruth wrote, "He was exalted. They had done it.

Now at last everyone must understand. And there would be no second world war."

There was more to come in the bombing tests—the use of new weapons in night attacks against an old American battleship, the *Alabama*—and there would be mock attacks on New York, Philadelphia and other eastern cities. But to the country, Mitchell's triumph was complete. Not even the official report, signed by General Pershing as chairman of the Joint Army-Navy Board, cooled the public's enthusiasm. People did not seem to notice, as Mitchell did with such anxiety, that the Board had said, "The battleship is still the backbone of the fleet and the bulwark of the nation's sea defense and will so remain so long as safe navigation of the sea for purposes of trade or transportation is vital to success in war."

Mitchell reacted strongly and "leaked" his own secret report on the tests to newspapers in violation of orders, taking the first step toward his eventual court martial. Then he said goodby to his squadrons, regretfully sending them back to their stations, where there was no bombing practice and little thought of preparing for a future war. Mitchell wrote, "Sorrowfully we broke up this splendid little air force. Never again except after another war shall we have such experience and efficiency."

Almost as if he wanted to forget, he flew to New York for the opening game of the World Series of 1921. Pearl Harbor was twenty years and two months away.

THE YOUNG SOLDIER

Billy Mitchell was destined for a brilliant career from boyhood. He was the son of a wealthy senator from Wisconsin and his parents encouraged him from infancy to be independent and self-reliant. The Mitchells were a strong-willed and unpredictable clan of Scotch descent, and from birth young Billy was one of the most remarkable of them.

He was born in December, 1879, in Nice, France, while his parents, Mr. and Mrs. John L. Mitchell, were on a European tour. He was the first of ten children, seven of whom were girls. Billy was three years old when he returned to the United States. He spoke French as naturally as English, and was also trained in German, Spanish and Italian. Back home, on a large farm called Meadowmere on the outskirts of Milwaukee, Billy and his brothers and sisters were brought up with thoroughbred horses, fine hunting dogs and prize farm animals.

Mitchell's grandfather, Alexander Mitchell, who founded

the family fortune, arrived from Scotland, a poor young bank clerk, in 1839 when Milwaukee was a frontier village. He became president of a large bank and of the longest rail system in the world, the 5000-mile Chicago, St. Paul and Milwaukee. His bank became so influential in the midwest that "Mitchell money" was a symbol of sound currency. Alexander Mitchell served two terms in Congress and for many years was one of the leading citizens of Wisconsin. His wife was deeply interested in American history and was one of the three women who founded the group which saved Mount Vernon and made George Washington's home a national shrine.

Billy's father, John Mitchell, was less interested in business than in politics, literature and art, and experimental farming. He filled his large house at Meadowmere with paintings and sculpture and fine furnishings from many countries. John Mitchell was an artillery officer during the Civil War but was discharged because of weak eyes.

Young Billy was small but wiry and absolutely fearless. He was also the despair of his Scotch governess who complained that "he absolutely never stopped." One of Billy's favorite pranks, which he performed almost daily, was to climb atop the farm's greenhouse, where he was forbidden to go, and walk across its roof so sure-footedly that he never fell or broke a pane of glass. He was five years old when he was given his first air rifle, and during an illness with scarlet fever about this time he shot at targets on the wall of his room. The room had to be redecorated.

Billy lived with guns for the rest of his life. He often hunted and camped alone in the Wisconsin woods and shot and stuffed more than two hundred native birds with the help of a well-known naturalist, Carl Akeley. Billy also rode horses on the farm's racetrack, helped to milk the cows, and played pirate in rowboats on a large pond.

His mother was the greatest influence of his early years, a forceful and dignified woman who controlled her children by a glance or a quiet word of caution. She taught Billy to be courageous and to do his duty when he was quite small. One day he came home discouraged and dirty after trying to ride a stubborn pony and complained, "Mummy, I can't handle that nasty beast."

"Then you go on riding it until you can," his mother said.

Billy learned. He was playing polo when he was thirteen years old and before he reached manhood had broken or dislocated most of his bones and joints.

Billy was an unusual student. In the first grade he spoke his native French for a few days, but other boys laughed at him and called him "Froggie," and he did not speak another word of French for many years. He went to a nearby prep school, Racine College, where he was normally a good student, but was sometimes charged with "boisterous conduct and disorder." In his letters home he asked for books that interested few other students in his school—works on electricity and physics. He also begged for a magnet and frequently made experiments which were not described in his text books. He became an avid amateur photographer, began a diary, and developed the habit of corresponding widely which was to be lifelong.

The Mitchell family lost much of its wealth during a severe business depression in the early 1890's when Billy's father insisted upon paying all depositors the money they had placed in the family bank, though many other banks closed at this time. This payment cost John Mitchell more than $1,350,000, and life at Meadowmere became less luxurious than before.

John Mitchell's name was placed in nomination as a candidate for Vice President at a Democratic Convention. He was elected to Congress and then to the Senate, where he became a pioneer in liberal social legislation. His opponents called him "wildly visionary" because he backed such schemes as the income tax and the eight-hour day for working men. He outraged other bankers by supporting the monetary program of William Jennings Bryan, who ran for President on the issue of allowing unlimited coinage of silver and rigid control of gold.

The Mitchells now moved to Washington, where Billy was still a trial to his governess, Mary Alexander. Mrs. Mitchell enrolled him in a dancing school, and when Mary tried to force him to attend, Billy hid his slippers; when he was sent without them he carried pockets full of frogs and caused havoc in the school. "Very rarely," when he had been on his good behavior, Billy was allowed to have dinner with important guests of the family; he joined in the conversation and chattered away with an air of supreme confidence.

Mrs. Mitchell encouraged this, developing the "quaint little Mitchell minds" by having all children advance their own opinions about everything. One famous politician who dined with the Mitchells one evening never forgot the scene in which all of the children performed their specialties—reciting, singing, or dancing. Mary Alexander played the zither as a finale.

Billy began to acquire a sense of American history. He often went with his grandmother to Washington's home at Mount Vernon, and Capitol Hill, which had been his playground for so long, seemed like a personal possession to him. His sister, Ruth, who was near his own age, noticed that when Billy said the word "America," his voice became deep with emotion. He was fascinated by the talk of the older Mitchells at home—of great American historic events, or the life of grandfather Mitchell, or of the new excitements then stirring in Congress where his father was so much involved. Ruth Mitchell thought her brother was strongly influenced by these discussions: "All this enterprise, integrity and enthusiasm was . . . the very air we breathed. America, its inspiring past and glowing future, became the very warp and woof of Bill's mind."

Senator Mitchell had become a pacifist, now struggling for peace as some of his fellow Senators began to urge war against Spain. But he was fascinated by old battles, especially those of the Civil War in which he had fought, and veterans of that war were frequently in his home.

When the family went to Europe one summer, the Senator dragged his children to many "dreary, once-gory old battlefields," much to the disgust of his daughters. But though the girls were bored, Billy was always bright-eyed and eager to hear more. He remembered for the rest of his life a visit to a village on the French coast in Normandy, where his father pointed dramatically across the English Channel and said, "This is the spot from which William the Conqueror sailed for England in the year 1066—the very last time that England was invaded. The very last time that an armed enemy ever set foot on English soil." Billy imagined that he could hear the grating of French longboats on the sand and the clanking of swords, shields and armor. He also delighted in a visit to Waterloo.

The summer's travels whetted Billy's appetite for historical reading, and he devoured books on the past. He was not the best of scholars, but when he read books of his own choosing he seemed to forget nothing. Ruth said that he knew *The Travels of Marco Polo* almost by heart.

Back home, there was a powerful movement toward war with Spain, and John Mitchell became one of its most outspoken opponents. He challenged those who wanted a declaration of war, saying that American policy in Cuba, Puerto Rico, Hawaii and the Philippines was shameful: "Europe already questions our sincerity in the declaration touching Cuba . . . the seizure of Hawaii would remove any doubt as to our all-around land-grabbing intentions. Since the advent of the white man every leaf in the history of Hawaii is either red with blood or black with intrigue."

On the eve of the Spanish-American War Senator Mitchell made a last stirring appeal to the nation's conscience: "No soldier should be mustered in for the purpose of shooting our ideas of liberty and justice into an alien people." The appeal went unheard.

After the sinking of the battleship *Maine* in Havana harbor, Senator Mitchell saw that it was useless to resist the clamor for revenge and said, "There are some things worse than war."

The Senator's son, Billy, became an enthusiastic young soldier without his father's consent. Billy, who was now eighteen and a junior in college, was in the Senate gallery when a declaration of war was passed. He ran home, packed his clothes and announced that he was off to Wisconsin to join his father's old regiment. When the defeated pacifist, Senator Mitchell, came home and saw Billy ready for war, he surprised the family by giving his consent. "He's eighteen and sound physically and mentally. I'd rather have them under twenty than over forty, if I were running a war."

As Billy left for Florida with his regiment an old friend

watched and then reported his departure to his family:

"I soon recognized him by a certain swing to his walk and the extreme badness of his hat—the very worst hat I ever saw. He gave a shy little jerk of his hand in response to our frantic handkerchief wavings. We just . . . laughed and joked and pretended it was all a picnic . . . and so we left him—gay and debonair—a typical soldier boy off to the wars."

Billy Mitchell had begun a distinguished career of twenty-eight years in the army, from which he was to be driven in the most sensational military controversy of his era, a storm that he was to brew himself.

3

"I AM NATURALLY
A SORT OF SOLDIER"

Within a few days after he joined the army in Florida, Mitchell became a second lieutenant, the youngest officer in uniform. He was appalled by the slovenly camps and complained that poor sanitation caused epidemics of typhoid fever and malaria. He wrote home, "Our latrines, garbage cans and trash heaps are stacked up beside the company kitchens. Can you imagine that? There are flies that have been here for months and know more about military drill and procedure than we do. When mess call rings out, they swarm off garbage heaps, do 'squads left,' and head straight for the mess shack and form up on our food . . . of the original nine men in my tent, only three of us have stayed out of hospital."

He fretted as the weeks passed and his unit was not sent into the fighting. He finally reached Cuba when war had ended and the island was taken over by the Americans. In the peace settlement the United States bought the Philippines for $20 million, and Puerto Rico and the island of

Guam in the Pacific also came under American control.

Mitchell won his first commendation for leading his Signal Corps troops on a march into the Cuban interior, a report that was praised for its clarity and breadth of expert knowledge. But he was restless. He saw that the natives hated the North Americans, though they had at first welcomed them. He also found the United States Army badly organized. "I really do believe that if we had been up against a first-rate power, they would have whaled the mischief right out of us." Billy remained in Cuba, stringing telegraph lines, until early in 1899 when a rebellion broke out in the Philippines. This insurrection was led by Emilio Aguinaldo, a guerrilla chief who fought the United States Army from jungle and mountain fastnesses, and Billy longed to join the struggle.

Mitchell used all of his ingenuity in an effort to get orders to the Pacific—even offering to give up his commission and fight as a private. He wrote his father, "Here I have been since the war without any foreign service to speak of and have not been in any engagements as yet. How would you have felt in the Civil War if you had been out of the way somewhere?" His father's influence was soon felt. Mitchell was ordered to the Philippines.

Billy was still nineteen when he passed through the United States on his way to Manila, and his proud father thought that the army had made a man of him. The Senator wrote his wife, "He stands straight and talks straight and, I may say, entertainingly. The impression he has made here on everybody is very favorable." Young Mitchell spent a few days in Milwaukee, where he saw his old friend Douglas MacArthur, whose father commanded a division in the Philippines. When he was warned that he would be thrown into the jungle fighting immediately,

Billy said, "It can't be too soon for me. That's why I joined up."

Less than two days after he landed at Manila Mitchell was on his way into battle with General Arthur MacArthur's troops, and when two American columns became separated in the jungles, Mitchell was ordered to link them with a telegraph line. He had almost no equipment, but Mitchell was not to be denied. He found cannon captured from the insurgents which had been wrapped with wire, and had that unwound. He stripped the country of barbed wire, improvised batteries by using table salt as a substitute for the prescribed chemical, sal ammoniac. Broken bottles and pieces of bamboo were used as insulators. His line produced a current so weak that Mitchell could detect it only by touching his tongue to the wire and holding a hand on the muddy earth. He could hear faintly the messages sent by dots and dashes. It was enough.

Billy led his company in stringing the line seventy-five miles through hostile country, hauling equipment with a herd of commandeered water buffalo. To discourage jungle tribesmen from making ornaments of his wire, he left a grim warning in each village: If the line broke, he would return to burn huts and kill cattle. Natives thereafter kept the line in repair. When Mitchell reached the distant column and established contact, general officers praised his makeshift telegraph line as a miracle.

Billy had won a major victory—for the old-line army officers in the United States were trying to persuade Congress to abolish the Signal Corps, with its new-fangled telegraph, saying that couriers on horseback would always be the best means of communication in battle. By the end of the campaign against the Philippine rebels, the army had used 16,000 miles of wire, much of it strung by Mitchell's company. The company also took part in the fighting and captured more than seventy insurgent flags. It was not civilized warfare—Mitchell frequently found the headless bodies of men butchered by Aguinaldo's guerrillas.

Mitchell's resourcefulness developed rapidly in this savage campaign. He had no watches, so he made a sundial for use by day, and hour glasses of two sand-filled bottles for use at night. When his horses lost shoes, he had them made from iron obtained from native villages. His men could erect huts within half an hour. When there were no roads for his carts, his men carried supplies in packs. As Billy wrote home, "We can make anything from gunpowder to telegraph instruments if necessary."

Billy liked the Filipinos and predicted that they would end the rebellion once they understood that the Americans did not come as conquerors. But he grew more critical of army policy and protested strict control of army troops from distant Washington. "We are told to go and do, with our hands tied behind our backs, our feet in a quagmire, and our mouths sealed when one word will release them. . . . I don't care to write this sort of stuff more than you like to read it."

Mitchell caught malaria, and the disease seemed to depress him. He wrote his mother, who was then traveling in Germany, that he wanted to leave the army, own a home, and have "some settled aim" in life. But he also saw the promise of future action in uniform. He forecast the opening of the World War by Germany. "There will be a big stir-up one of these days . . . and probably with the country in which you now are."

Mitchell left the Philippines on a long leave, but instead of resigning he volunteered for duty in Alaska, where, after many failures, the army hoped to link the interior and the coast by telegraph. For the next two winters, in weather often seventy degrees below zero, Mitchell drove his men and dog teams across the forbidding country, in snows sometimes forty feet deep—until he had completed a telegraph line 1700 miles long. He was promoted to captain for his work in Alaska, and he had overcome his malaria, but more important, he had found a new interest to which he would devote his life—aviation. For many weeks, while snowbound in Alaskan cabins, he and a companion pored over books on aeronautics, soaking up the limited information about two men who had so recently flown, Otto Lilienthal, a German glider expert, and Professor Samuel P. Langley, an American who was attempting power flights.

Billy returned to the United States, convinced that his future lay with the army. He told his father, "If I ever get a chance in the field I think that I can do something . . . I am naturally a sort of soldier." He was married soon after his return in 1903, to Caroline Stoddard of Rochester, New York, and his bride laughingly complained that even on their honeymoon in Mexico, Billy was more interested in warfare than in his wife. She noted that he constantly played a game in which he actually seemed to see guns blazing and troops moving across the landscape; every day, he studied Mexican terrain for good artillery positions.

The next year, on duty at Fort Leavenworth, Kansas, Mitchell experimented with the army's first field radio stations, and by using a kite that carried wire 10,000 feet into the air, he received a radio signal from Puerto Rico, 1900 miles away. He also worked with photography from kites, with the rapid processing of photographs in the field—and by the time he was twenty-five, had written a text book on communications. He was still looking into the future. Only three years after the first feeble flight of the Wright brothers, Billy predicted in an army magazine, "Conflicts no doubt will be carried on in the future in the air, on the surface of the earth and water, and under the water."

The next six years passed swiftly for Mitchell, in army schools and on duty in distant posts. He was rushed to San Francisco after the city was rocked by a great earthquake, he was back in Cuba during a native uprising, then returned to the United States to become the first Signal Corps officer to graduate from the Army's School of The Line. His commanding officers praised him in their reports of these years. "Captain Mitchell is an earnest, zealous, efficient young officer, intensely interested in his professional work . . . agreeable, courteous, cheerful . . . will undertake to accomplish anything; ambitious and willing."

In 1909 Billy was sent back to the Philippines, where the rebellion had ended. He was now the father of two daughters. He played polo expertly and was captain of the Army team that won the Eastern Cup in Hong Kong. This carefree life on army posts was interrupted in 1910 when Mitchell volunteered for a spy mission, a long trip by boat through the small islands lying off the Philippines. He found many Japanese there, operating wireless stations, apparently reporting on every move of the Americans in the Philippines. Billy was a clever spy, posing as a naturalist and photographing freely without arousing suspicion. He reported to Washington, "The Japanese were at first very distant . . . but as they are quite lonely, beer and cigarettes . . . had an immediate effect." He was allowed to sketch and photograph in the islands undisturbed.

Mitchell continued his spying in 1911, traveling through Japan and Manchuria, from where he sent reports, complete with photographs and samples of field wire used by the Japanese army. He described new Japanese rifle sights and the work of engineers, medical corps and all other branches of the army. From China, Mitchell reported that though the country was badly disorganized, "Before many years they will be able to take care of themselves. . . . If the uncounted millions of Chinese could be organized, equipped and led properly . . . there is nothing they could not accomplish." Billy reviewed the 20,000 crack troops of the Chinese war lord, Chang Tso-Lin, and was impressed by their skill and vigor.

The most prophetic of his observations from the Orient —thirty years before Pearl Harbor—was buried in one of these reports which was soon gathering dust in army files in Washington. "Increasing friction between Japan and the United States will take place in the future . . . this will lead to war sooner or later." He saw indications that this war of the future might be fought in the air, for the Japanese were fascinated by aviation. Even schoolboys in the city of Kyoto flew five-foot models of planes and attracted great crowds of spectators.

Mitchell was called back from Japan to be honored as one of the Army's most promising young officers. At the age of thirty-two he had been chosen to serve on the General Staff, the youngest man ever selected. Billy wrote his mother, "I may be a general before many years have passed." He settled in Washington with his family, riding in horse shows and hunts, playing tennis and sailing on the Potomac, as if he were living the normal life of a staff officer prominent in capital society.

But behind the scenes Mitchell spent his days in Intelligence, a place he had won by his reports from the Far East. He glimpsed new worlds. Europe was now racked by the prelude to world war, with the outbreak of the Balkan Wars. Across Mitchell's desk flowed reports on new weapons—Bulgarian pilots flew over Turkish cities dropping small bombs. The Greeks tried to bomb warships in the Dardanelles, the first attempt of its kind. Mitchell saw that European nations were outstripping the United States in developing aviation. Americans had flown the first power-driven plane and invented the machine gun, and been first to land a plane on a warship—but now the United States Army had only six fragile planes. The French were said to have 1200, most of them ready for battle. Mitchell was aroused; he determined to learn more about war in the air.

At the army's new flying school at College Park, Maryland, he met Lieutenant H.H. (Hap) Arnold, who was to become United States air commander in World War II. In the summer of 1912 Arnold was trying to fashion the plane into a weapon, practicing bombing, flying to great heights —he had recently set a new record of 4674 feet—and firing machine guns from the air. Arnold was impressed by Mitchell and remembered the meeting for many years. "His questions about the air were intelligent and to the point . . . he did most of the talking, asking questions only to get concrete facts."

Billy was still three years away from his first plane ride, but he quickly became an aviation expert and was called to testify before Congress on developing European air power. He was asked to draft legislation for the army's development in the air. Very soon afterward, Mitchell's new standing as a consultant on aviation became important. In July, 1914, German columns marched into the Low Countries and crossed the French border and the World War was on. In Washington, Mitchell gave daily briefings to

Congressmen, and it was through him that the legislators got their views of the war's opening phases.

His study of the German military machine impressed Mitchell, but it also alarmed him. He was one of the first Americans to sound this alarm: "People who have not studied the German organization in every line do not appreciate what a wonderful and coordinated empire it is, both for war and in peace. We may run up against it before many years are over, or against an almost equally well organized one, Japan."

Billy dared the anger of superiors to make public his fears of American unpreparedness when he spoke to a group of engineers in Washington. Newspaper headlines got him into trouble, his first brush with the army's high command:

SAYS FOE CAN TAKE U.S.
ERE ARMY IS RAISED

Capt. Mitchell, U.S. Army General
Staff, Gives Startling Military Facts

When he was called to account, Mitchell defended himself stoutly, submitted copies of his speech and said he was misquoted. He was warned against further criticism, and the army also announced a stern policy—no officer could air his opinions publicly, whatever his views on national defense.

This seemed to inspire Mitchell to perfect his criticisms, and he submitted a report whose title was enough to enrage veteran officers—"Our Faulty Military Policy." Mitchell's paper urged the creation of a Council of National Defense, with control over the fiercely independent Army and Navy. "We would then," he said, "have the whole national defense brains, so to speak, under one roof." He urged compulsory military service as the one practical system for a democracy. He also warned that, because of the submarine and the plane, the United States was no longer safe from enemy attack. Most outrageous of all, the generals thought, was his final criticism: "The military policy of the United States is and has been to prepare for war *after such war has actually broken out.*"

The General Staff began to have its doubts about the promising young officer and these were reflected in his annual fitness reports. "Very capable, alert. I consider him better suited to active service with troops than on General Staff duty. . . . Especially fitted for field service." Headquarters had begun to wish that Mitchell were somewhere else—anywhere else; it was to become a persistent yearning.

Mitchell left the General Staff; now a major, he was thirty-six years old. He set out to learn to fly.

The nearest army flying school was in Newport News, Virginia, operated by the early plane builder, Glenn Curtiss. Mitchell went there with a veteran pilot, Tom Milling, who gave him his first flight. "He was crazy about it," Milling said. Billy went down faithfully every weekend and paid his own way, including a large bill of almost $1500 for his lessons in an old Jenny. Billy's instructor, Jimmy Johnson, found him self-confident and quick to learn, but refused to allow him to solo after a few brief flights. One day when Johnson was ill, Mitchell persuaded his substitute, Walter Lees, to let him fly alone. He made two solo flights the first day without mishap—but when Johnson returned, and Mitchell insisted on another solo trip, there was a crash.

Mitchell leveled off too high as he landed, plopped

down on the rough unpaved runway and flipped the Jenny on its back. Johnson rushed to the plane and found Mitchell hanging upside down in the cockpit. "Are you all right?"

Mitchell said only, "What did I do wrong?"

Billy wrote later of the crash, "It taught me more than anything that ever happened to me in the air." He flew each weekend for five months and by January, 1917, he had fifteen hours of instruction. He began to badger the army to send him to France where, he was positive, the United States would soon be involved in war. His friend Hap Arnold thought the Army was glad to see Billy go, because of his sharp criticisms of the command.

Billy got permission to leave in March, "for the specific purpose of observing the manufacture and development of aircraft," and to study French methods of fighting an air war. He was on his way to Paris, passing through neutral Spain, when America entered the war on April 6, 1917. Mitchell soon reached the front, the first United States officer in uniform under fire.

"THE PRINCE
OF THE AIR"

Mitchell went to work eagerly in Paris, as if he sensed that the conflict between Germany and the Allies was to usher in a new day of warfare, and as if he foresaw that he was to emerge as one of the most celebrated of its veterans.

Within less than a month after his arrival, Mitchell became the first United States flier to cross enemy lines, and newspaper headlines back home made him the most popular of American war heroes.

A few days later Billy was taking lessons from Victor Fumat, a leading instructor of French fighter pilots, and the moment he left the ground in an agile Nieuport, he realized that his criticisms had been more accurate than he knew. America was hopelessly behind in aviation.

"I had been able to flounder around with the animated kites that we called airplanes in the United States, but when I laid my hand to the greyhounds of the air they had in Europe, which went twice as fast as ours, it was an en-

tirely different matter." Within a month of intensive training, Mitchell qualified as a Junior Military Aviator, the
highest ranking open to him. It was his last instruction in
flying.

Billy began a bombardment of Washington, urging that
the United States buy or build French planes—Spads,
Nieuports and Breguets, which were meeting the best of
the German planes over the front. He was soon off on an
extended tour of the battle zone, where he inspected and
photographed everything and hurried his reports to Washington. He took part in an infantry attack against the Germans, waited in dugouts under artillery bombardments,
and wrote home proudly that he was the first American in
United States uniform and on duty to go under enemy fire.
He won a Croix de Guerre from the French for this action.
He was fascinated by the first tanks he had seen; he also
noted the French Army's expertness in camouflage, battlefield photography, bridge building, anti-aircraft fire, use of
searchlights, and meteorology for its aviation. Billy also
began to write of the French concept of massed air power,
the need for concentrating flights of hundreds of bombers
and fighters against the enemy, rather than wasting them
in piecemeal attacks.

One flight over the fighting front gave Mitchell a clearer
idea of the positions of the armies than weeks of traveling
on the ground. "A very significant thing to me," he said,
"was that we could cross the lines of these contending armies in a few minutes in our airplane, whereas the armies
had been locked in the struggle, immovable, powerless to
advance, for three years. . . . It was as though they kept
knocking their heads against a stone wall, until their
brains were dashed out. They got nowhere, as far as end-
ing the war was concerned. It looked as though the war

would keep up indefinitely until either the airplanes brought an end to the war or the contending nations dropped from sheer exhaustion."

He was convinced that the plane could end the bloody stalemate which was already three years old. Mitchell was chosen to prepare for the arrival of United States airmen in the coming months. There was no money, but Mitchell opened an office anyway, borrowing rooms from an American firm, spending his own money, and asking contributions from United States civilians. He sent an urgent cable, asking the army for $50,000 to establish the American air program. After a long silence he was told that it was "not customary" to entrust so much money to a junior officer. A lieutenant on Mitchell's volunteer staff retorted, "It is not customary to have a world war."

Mitchell was invited to lecture to the French Senate on war in the air and gave an impressive résumé, including a promise of American participation, which was not far away. By the time General John J. Pershing arrived with his staff to direct the enormous American Expeditionary Force, Mitchell was a lieutenant colonel, and was deep in the work of the Inter-Allied Board, which was to produce planes for the American squadrons. Mitchell and his French friends conceived a plan for the United States to furnish twenty thousand planes and forty thousand mechanics and had this demand sent to Washington by Premier Ribot. American officials were stunned. The United States Air Service then had fifty-two officers, eleven hundred men, two hundred civilian mechanics—and no combat planes. Still, Mitchell's scheme formed the basis of a new policy under which the United States furnished an air force three times the size of the French.

By now Mitchell had also toured the British front and

learned his first lessons in strategic air power from Sir Hugh Trenchard, who commanded the 2000-plane Royal Air Force. Trenchard at first thought Mitchell brash and cocksure, but after a few of the American's insistent questions, he said, "Come along, young man. I can see you're the sort who usually gets what he wants in the end."

Trenchard explained his operations from headquarters maps and traced the evolution of the air war against the Germans, which had begun with pilots dropping darts on enemy soldiers below and had advanced to long-range bombing against industrial centers. When he saw night bomber squadrons taking off for distant German cities, Mitchell was convinced. "This is the proper way to use air power, and I am sure the future will see operations conducted in this way by thousands of airplanes."

Mitchell found that the British were less tradition-bound than the French and were quicker to try new weapons. He saw the importance of this attitude. "The great captains are those who thought out new methods and then put them into execution," he said. "Anybody can always use the old methods. That is the trouble with old regular army officers; they can never get out of the rut, but always go into a war with the methods of a former war . . . sure to be whipped whenever they run up against an elastic-minded, constructive leader on the other side."

Trenchard followed Mitchell's busy career for the next few months as he battled his way through the confusion of organizing the United States air arm, and said, "Mitchell is a man after my own heart. If only he can break his habit of trying to convert opponents by killing them, he'll go far."

It was more than a year after the American declaration of war that Pershing reviewed the first of his divisions to arrive in Paris. The French gave a wildly joyous greeting to the first of the American infantrymen who had come to help drive back the German invaders, but on that day Mitchell made a melancholy entry in his diary: "Our air force consists of one Nieuport plane which I use myself, and that is all." He was soon locked in a bitter struggle for both the creation of an air force and for its command.

Unaware that Mitchell had been sent to Paris, Pershing arrived with an air officer of his own, Major T.F. Dodd. The major was a veteran pilot, but since Mitchell outranked him, he became aviation officer at headquarters. Mitchell soon discovered that this meant nothing. A procession of aviation commissions and experts soon began arriving from Washington, bringing conflicting orders and opinions that threatened to overwhelm the Air Service. It was through Dodd, in these days, that Mitchell met one of his greatest fliers. On a tour of the front with French officers, Mitchell's car broke down on the road, and the party was marooned until Dodd drove up and had his chauffeur work on the balky motor. Within a few minutes repairs were made, and Mitchell was on his way. The chauffeur, he learned, was a champion racetrack driver, Eddie Rickenbacker. Mitchell encouraged him to become a flying student, and Rickenbacker became the leading American ace.

By now the first official mission had come from the United States to study combat aviation, train a few American mechanics, and return with a plan for organizing an air force. The mission set up a system of bases and flying schools to support American fighting squadrons, of which there were none by the spring of 1918. American pilots flew only in French squadrons as volunteers. This mission resulted in the decision to build one type of plane in the

United States, a British two-seater light bomber which Mitchell thought worthless. It was to be powered by a new engine known as the Liberty. Mitchell protested that the engine would not suit the plane, and that money was being wasted and time lost, and charged English manufacturers with lobbying to promote the scheme. He wrote his mother, "I suppose that aviation after my departure from the States was handled worse than anything ever has been."

Billy was also irritated by the coming and going of staff officers. "Few of them had ever been to Europe," he said, "and most of them were thinking more about rank for themselves than what to do with the troops . . . they were full of information as to what should and should not be done."

The source of most trouble, Mitchell thought, was the Commander-in-Chief. "General Pershing himself thought aviation was full of dynamite and pussyfooted just when he needed the most action. . . . We were running into more and more trouble with our own staff about aviation matters. It was such a big subject and ignorance about it was so widespread that each member had to be told, from the bottom up, whenever anything new occurred . . . . Incoming papers were passed around from one section to another, just as in Washington, with everyone trying to avoid responsibility."

For months quarrels within the General Staff vexed Mitchell and others who were trying to get United States squadrons into action. "It was terrible to have to fight with an organization of this kind," he said, "instead of devoting all our attention to the powerful enemy in our front." He sometimes argued hotly with Pershing and both men shouted and pounded the table with their fists. Pershing once threatened to send Mitchell home if he continued to insist on having his way with the air force.

"If you do, you'll soon come after me," Mitchell said. Pershing laughed, and their talk ended on a friendly note, but Billy's troubles were not over. Pershing made General William Kenly chief of the Air Service, and a few months later, when the experienced aviator, General Benjamin Foulois, arrived, Pershing placed him in command. Mitchell and Foulois fought over Air Service policy, even though Mitchell was in command at the front, and Foulois in the rear areas. Mitchell scorned his new chief and other newcomers:

"While Foulois meant well and had some experience in aviation in the United States, he was not at all conversant with conditions in Europe. As rapidly as possible the competent men, who had learned their duties in the face of the enemy, were displaced and their positions taken by these carpetbaggers . . . a shipload of aviation officers . . . almost none of whom had ever seen an airplane. A more incompetent lot of air warriors had never arrived in the zone of active military operations."

Foulois asked Pershing to send Mitchell to the United States because of his "extremely childish attitude," saying that he was "mentally unfitted for further field service."

Pershing settled the squabble by calling on an old West Point classmate, General Mason Patrick, a stern Engineer officer. Patrick learned of his new assignment from the exasperated commander in these words: "In all of this Army, there is but one thing causing me real anxiety, and that's the Air Service. There are a lot of good men in it, but they're running around in circles. Somebody has got to make them go straight. I want you to do the job." Patrick had never been in a plane, but he began at once to still the noisy Air Service and improve its "chaotic condition of affairs."

Mitchell gladly escaped the staff battles for action at the front, where his first patrols were flown in April, 1918. Two inexperienced American pilots, Lieutenants Douglas Campbell and Alan Winslow, won the opening victory against the powerful German air force. When enemy planes were reported in the cloudy skies, Campbell and Winslow took off in their French Spads. They were just gaining altitude when two German fighters appeared. The Americans dived at them, Winslow shot down one plane and Campbell the other, and the veteran German pilots parachuted to the ground where they were captured. The first of Mitchell's victories had been won in four and a half minutes. A cheering crowd of pilots and ground crewmen welcomed Campbell and Winslow back to their field, and the thrilling news of the remarkable dogfight against the German fliers spread quickly among French civilians, so long depressed by invasion, defeat, and the ravaging of their country. Other victories in the air followed rapidly on Mitchell's front, with the French 8th Army between the Meuse and Moselle rivers. His leading pilots became the most renowned men in the Allied armies, and Rickenbacker, Campbell, Raoul Lufbery and Harold Hartney soon became aces.

Mitchell also assembled a staff and command of brilliant, unorthodox and daring men, officers of a new breed, many of whom were to become leaders of American aviation. He installed his old friend Tom Milling, now a colonel, as his Chief of Staff. Colonel Lewis Brereton, an observation pilot, became chief of the attack squadrons; Hartney led a pursuit squadron. Millard F. Harmon, Clayton

Bissell, and Elmer Haslett also became Mitchell's aides. There was also a less accomplishd officer whom Mitchell used shrewdly, a headquarters guinea pig to whom Mitchell read each order. "If he could understand them, anybody could," Mitchell said. "He wasn't particularly bright, but he was one of my most valuable officers for that reason."

Despite enormous handicaps, Mitchell's small force won its surprising victories, day after day, as the summer of 1918 wore on. There were still no American planes in France—and none were to come. Mitchell appealed to the Allied commander, Marshal Foch, for new Spads when he found that his worn-out Nieuports were no match for the big, swift squadrons of Baron von Richthofen's Flying Circus. A few British bombers joined Mitchell and began striking at the enemy rear, forcing the Germans to adopt new tactics to protect ammunition dumps and troop concentrations.

Mitchell's success won praise even from his adversary at headquarters, Foulois, who reported to Pershing that he found a "high fighting spirit of morale" in the squadrons, and a most efficient supervision of battle training, supply and all else on the front. The Air Service became an effective fighting unit just as the Germans launched their last great offensive of the war, striking across the Marne toward Paris. Mitchell himself discovered the strength and direction of the attack. He went up alone on his daring flight, without protection, and without telling his headquarters where he was going. He flew along the Marne on the foggy morning of July 15, 1918, into the battle area where seventy German divisions were on the move.

"Suddenly as I rounded a turn of the river east of Dormans," he reported, "I saw a great mass of artillery fire hitting the south bank, and, spanning the river, five bridges filled with German troops marching over."

There were no German planes about, and Mitchell flew to within five hundred feet of the enemy columns. "Looking down on the men, marching so splendidly, I thought to myself, what a shame to spoil such fine infantry."

Mitchell reported the German advance to First Army headquarters, and his planes soon joined American infantry and artillery in the counter-attack against the Germans. One of his pilots saw that Mitchell's flight and report had been the work of "a rare tactician and strategist" who saw what other officers could not. "He realized the awful truth where the ordinary airman would not have conceived the possibilities . . . when the fliers found out who had made that mysterious flight, our morale was strengthened one hundred per cent."

Air losses were heavy in the battle for Château-Thierry and though Mitchell knew the squadrons had fought well, he said that "many things were left to be desired." He was already planning a radically new kind of air war, in which he could gain mastery of an entire battle front. He began to call for a fleet of fifteen hundred Allied planes, British, French and Italian. No such air force had ever been assembled, but with the aid of Pershing and Foch, Mitchell gathered the enormous fleet near the front at St. Mihiel, where a German salient thrust deep into the Allied line—and where another fierce battle was in the making.

In early September the big new American army moved toward the horseshoe-shaped salient at St. Mihiel, more than 400,000 troops with 3000 cannon in line. It was to straighten the Allied line by driving the Germans from this shell-pocked and trench-scarred landscape that had become a desert in four years of stalemated war. Some of the first United States tanks were now moving into battle, led by Mitchell's young friend Lieutenant Colonel George S. Patton, Jr.

As the infantry and artillery filled the roads, Mitchell scattered his vast new air force over fourteen fields, camouflaging his planes and continually moving dummy planes to deceive German scouts. He now had forty-nine squadrons, twenty-two of them American.

The British were led by General Trenchard, eight squadrons of night bombers assigned to hammer the German rear. Mitchell noted in his diary that there was no dissension: "Here we were, a force of four nations, acting together with no discord. . . . Such a thing could not have occurred with ground troops." He was ready with "the first definite American command organized for grand operations in our history."

Mitchell found Pershing cheerful and confident before the battle—and also more confident of his airmen. Mitchell wrote, "Our air people, who for a long time had felt that Pershing did not know, or care to know, very much about aviation, were beginning to change their minds, as he was helping us in every way possible. I guess he couldn't swallow the whole hog to begin with, had to take it easy."

Pershing and Foch approved Mitchell's plan of air support for the ground troops: he would drive the Germans from the air with sweeps of his planes, seal off the rear by bombing communications and marching troops, and cover allied infantry as it massed. Things were "going like clockwork," Mitchell reported, as he and his staff prepared for the first complete air battle. He wrote his mother proudly, as he had written her of his accomplishments since boyhood: "I am in a field of activity and command all air troops in service in our area. Someday I shall write and tell you about the number of airplanes. Should they fly at once the sky would be black."

Mitchell made his headquarters in a battered school building back of the lines, where he drilled squadron commanders in his plan of attack. Elmer Haslett first went to the place and found Mitchell and half a dozen others crawling on the floor around a huge relief map of the St. Mihiel area. "It was like toy-soldier stuff, but in deadly earnest." The map had been made in sections by French photographic balloons, and when assembled it revealed every rise and fold, every stream, building, hill and defensive position in the salient. Mitchell spent days over it: "This, combined with my intimate knowledge of the country . . . from flying over it with French and American observers . . . made me feel that I knew this part of the world as well as any man living."

On September 10 Mitchell flew alone over the lines and confirmed an Allied report that the Germans had begun to retreat before the great attack could be launched. He saw long columns of gray-green enemy infantry crawling on the muddy roads beneath him, and took his report to headquarters. He did not convince all ground officers. On the night before the attack Pershing held a conference at headquarters, and Mitchell was outraged when the chief engineer officer urged postponement. Billy fumed as this officer made endless objections—the rain would slow delivery of ammunition on the railroads, the roads would be almost impassable to trucks, and water could not be hauled up for the troops. "A thousand and one things which could not be done," as Mitchell said. He saw that several "old fossils" in the group were nodding agreement with the engineer. "You can always trust an engineer officer to go on the defensive whenever it's possible," Mitchell thought.

Pershing called on Mitchell last, as the junior officer present. Mitchell remembered it later: "I told them very plainly that I knew the Germans were withdrawing . . . as I had seen them personally . . . furthermore, I said, there wasn't going to be much of a battle at St. Mihiel, and our troops might be better off without artillery, as they might shoot a good many of our own men . . . all we had to do was to jump on the Germans, and the quicker we did it, the better." He was relieved when Pershing ordered the attack to open the next day on schedule.

The first day of St. Mihiel, September 12, was gray and rainy, and the crude airdromes were deep in mud, so that few squadrons got off to bomb the rear and strafe enemy positions. A future Air Force general, Major Carl (Tooey) Spaatz, a young Pennsylvanian, led his fifteen-plane squadron of Spads into a dogfight that day. Spaatz was shocked by the speed of the action. "The thing really happened so darned fast that the only recollection you have is diving on a plane, or seeing them try to dive on you, and you maneuver either to get away or get on them. I knocked down three Fokkers."

Another of Mitchell's pilots stood forlornly by his hangar, gazing out over his flooded runway, when he heard an incredible roar in the cloudy sky. A flight of six or seven hundred planes swarmed past beneath the low clouds. "I didn't believe my eyes, because we'd never seen such a thing before. I happened to be standing on the air field when this darned thing started to go over. Then it went and it went . . . it was awfully impressive." This pilot, Kenneth Littauer, managed to get his own plane into the air soon afterward and reported that Mitchell's flight had swept the sky clear of enemy aircraft.

Flying conditions were little better the next day, but the squadrons went aloft anyway. Men and planes were lost in crashes, but Mitchell controlled the sky over the battlefield. As he described the action, "I sent five hundred planes across like this, and as soon as they were over, five hundred more from this side, like a boxer, hitting right and left. We cut them off in the rear, deep along this line, and bombed their air dromes and roads and rail yards. We drove them out of the air. . . ."

The first day had decided the battle, with all objectives taken, and within four days the line had been straightened and the German air force driven from the area. The war had entered its final phase. Some allied infantrymen refused to believe that the airmen had played an important part at St. Mihiel—they scoffed at fliers as undisciplined rovers who flew where they wished, were seldom under fire, and never on hand when commanders needed them. Pershing was an old cavalryman who had never flown, but he saw the value of Mitchell's blows and sent him official congratulations for his handling of "the tremendous concentration of air forces," and praised "the courage and nerve shown by your officers . . . and the high morale which permeates the service under your command . . . I am proud of you all."

Mitchell was promoted to brigadier general and was awarded the French Legion of Honor, but there was little time for celebration. The airmen were thrown into battle once more. The Allies attacked with more than half a million men along the fifty-mile front of the Argonne, a long offensive which was to break German resistance. United

States industrial power and manpower had turned the tide, and was soon to bring allied victory and peace to Europe. Mitchell used his basic plan of St. Mihiel in the new battle, but his tactical problems were much more demanding. He was forced to strike across parallel battle lines open to flank attack.

His French squadrons moved back to their own army. British and American forces had grown, but except for a few DeHavilland "flying coffins" which carried many men to flaming death, there were still no American-built warplanes. Mitchell's pilots still flew the French Spads and Nieuports. He massed the squadrons in the center of the front and improved his communications by using radio, telephone and motorcycle couriers between airfields. The Germans were much stronger than at St. Mihiel, but Mitchell kept their planes off the United States infantry during most of the advance. He flew out himself almost daily. Once, when he spotted congested truck traffic at a village crossroads, he ordered a fleet of 320 bombers to strike nearby German positions to keep enemy squadrons busy—and had Hartney's pursuit planes to fly just above United States infantrymen to shield them from attack.

Newspaper correspondents who had found Mitchell's headquarters began telling Americans of the unfamiliar new pattern of the war. On the busiest day of the air offensive over the Argonne, sixty German planes and twelve balloons had been shot down, with a loss of about twenty Allied planes. Mitchell reported that one wing of his force had flown 45,000 miles that day, fought fifty combats and destroyed nineteen German planes without loss. He praised his pilots extravagantly: "There is nothing to beat them in the world."

In October, Mitchell was promoted to command of the

Air Service, Group of Armies, and Tom Milling succeeded him as air chief of the First Army. Mitchell was now one of the most popular men in France. Hap Arnold, who visited him, saw that the army's legends about the airman were not exaggerated. He was unorthodox in everything, including his unique uniforms. "He was on top of the world. . . . Laughing and constantly talking, wearing that blouse with the outside pockets and the famous pink breeches."

Mitchell was now almost thirty-nine years old, a spare, athletic figure weighing about one hundred-fifty pounds, five feet ten inches tall. He was quick and graceful, with a strikingly erect posture, more agile than many younger officers about him. His boyish face was dimpled, with a long sharp nose, cleft chin and charming smile. He had an air of vital energy and an infectious enthusiasm, especially when he talked of the promise of air power in keeping peace. He had spent twenty-one years in the army, fought in three wars, and had seen fourteen major engagements in France.

One of his pilots described him in these days: "He didn't walk like other men, and though he was modest and considerate of everybody, there was pride in every movement. Even if he had only eight or ten feet to walk, he went at it as though he were marching a mile, and was late. He moved at top speed."

Hap Arnold was impressed by the stream of fliers and ranking officers from other services at Mitchell's headquarters, come for a look at the hero of the aviators. "The fliers around him would have done anything for him," Arnold said, "and so would the boys out in the squadrons. . . . Billy was clearly The Prince of the Air now."

Arnold was thinking ahead to peacetime, when the

United States must build up its air power, and he urged Mitchell to return to Washington and become chief of the Air Service. "Why shouldn't you capitalize on your war record? Can you swing it with Pershing?" Mitchell declined. "I want to see this thing through," he said. When Germany surrendered, he would take his pilots across the Rhine with the army of occupation. Arnold did not give up. Above all others, he thought, Mitchell had the knowledge, experience, prestige and courage to build a great United States air force.

Only when the Armistice came in November did Mitchell realize that he had been living under almost unbearable strain for a year and a half. For the past six months he had slept no more than three hours a night. The daily reports from the squadrons did not reach him until 10 P.M., and his orders, based on the reports, went out at about 2 o'clock in the morning. By 5 A.M. he was up to watch the first of his planes depart.

On Armistice Day he went out to the airdromes to congratulate the squadron commanders: "This was the first time in world's history that great bodies of air troops have been brought together and fought as a single organization. We Americans have developed the best system of air fighting that the world has ever seen. . . . If our system is maintained, we can look forward to the future with absolute confidence. Our men who have been trained in combat must be put in charge, to make America absolutely safe from hostile invasion."

Mitchell made his way over crowded roads to Paris on Armistice night in a big Mercedes given to him by the French Government—and when he was recognized by some French pilots on the boulevards, he was surrounded by celebrants who "almost picked up the automobile" and towed it through the streets for most of the night. The next day, Pershing sent Mitchell into the German Ruhr as air commander of the army of occupation. He took with him a few of the most veteran squadrons and settled at airfields near Coblenz on the Rhine.

Mitchell accepted hundreds of new German planes in surrender, wrote his reports of the war's actions, visited other United States commands, and studied the German people. Suddenly, he tired of life in the remote post, and one day when he was called to headquarters to receive a medal from the French Marshal Petain, Mitchell asked to be sent home immediately. Pershing agreed and ordered Mitchell to go home by way of England, where he was to talk with General Trenchard and other air officers and study the independent British air command. Perhaps the United States should use this system.

Mitchell, inspected flying fields and aircraft plants over most of England, and was again impressed by the orderly British methods. "Everywhere the British are, there is system. . . . If we could have the air organization in the United States that the British have we would be so far ahead of the rest of the world that there would be no comparison."

Billy's sister Ruth, who was living in London, was surprised to see his plain blouse, with only a pair of silver wings on his chest. "Where are all those medals we've been hearing about?" Billy fished the Legion of Honor medal from a pocket. "Is that all?" He rather sheepishly pulled out the others—a Croix de Guerre with Palm, and the Italian Order of Sts. Maurice and Lazarus, the Victory Medal, with clasps for many battles—Cambrai, the Somme, Meuse-Argonne, Champagne-Marne, and the Distinguished Service Cross and Medal.

Mitchell talked with King George V and Winston Churchill during his visit and proposed closer relations between Great Britain and the United States. Then, after an absence of nearly two years, he boarded the liner *Aquitania* for home. He was not a typical homebound veteran.

Passengers were astonished to find Mitchell in a salon every day, lecturing to a group of officers who sat as if spellbound. The next war, he said, would be fought in the air. There would be no more static trench fighting, as in the World War, which had cost thirty-seven million casualties, eight million of them dead. In the future great fleets of planes would strike at factories and cities and not simply at armies. The first line of defense was now in the sky. Without air forces to shield them, armies and navies would be helpless. They must go home and wake up their countrymen. If the war had lasted a little longer, Mitchell said, he could have shown them a clear view of the military future.

He displayed photographs of fighting planes, diagrams of air battles, tables of organization for air forces, even Royal Air Force posters. His talk was all of war, and he did not mention the peace plans then holding the world's attention. President Woodrow Wilson was soon to leave the United States in an effort to build a permanent peace, but Mitchell spoke to his small audience as if he were confident that peace could be kept only if great nations armed to halt aggression.

Germany had surrendered too soon, he said, before she was actually defeated. "I wonder how long it will be before American troops must go back to Europe," Mitchell said.

His forceful, colorful speech amused spectators. "The General Staff knows as much about the air as a hog does about ice skating. . . . We've got a standing army that's stood too long. . . . The war's over. The generals in Washington got out of their swivel chairs and went over to watch, and they're going back to sit down again. They've learned nothing and forgotten nothing."

Mitchell was supremely confident but he realized that he faced a bitter struggle at home, before he convinced the American people that air power was vital to their future security; he did not doubt that he would win his battle in the end.

One officer who listened was a distinguished Navy plane designer, Jerome C. Hunsaker, who did not agree with all of Mitchell's theories. "Mitchell was intelligent, persuasive and good-tempered," he observed, "even when his assertions were objected to. He liked to try out some of these papers on me and the other passengers. He would give close attention to objections and criticisms."

But Hunsaker also saw that Mitchell would be a dangerous adversary. "He was a very attractive fellow . . . a politician in uniform. We, who were somewhat prejudiced, thought the cause was Billy Mitchell himself, and not air power." The thought was to be repeated often by Navy officers and Army ground officers in the hectic years ahead.

As the liner entered New York harbor, a flight of planes from nearby Mitchel Field made wide circles overhead. It was Mitchell's welcome home. As soon as he reached Washington, he was to become chief of Military Aeronautics, assigned to build an air force. In his dreams, Mitchell saw this as the greatest military power on earth, destined to defend the United States for generations, and to keep peace far into the future.

THE BATTLE FOR
AIR POWER BEGINS

Mitchell returned to Washington in March, 1919, to find the capital in a carefree mood. The country seemed to have put aside all thoughts of national defense with the signing of the Armistice. The future seemed to belong to America, and the public was weary of war and sacrifice. The army of 2,000,000 was to be disbanded overnight, as if its very existence embarrassed the United States. The country wanted only to enjoy the industrial boom stimulated by the war. It had almost no interest in the Army or Navy, and even less in aviation. Only a handful of Americans had yet flown, and none of Mitchell's superior officers had left the ground in a plane.

The Air Service, which had 20,000 officers, 2800 pilots and 150,000 enlisted men, was to be reduced to 1300 officers by the end of the year. Still, Mitchell began with serene confidence. He flew to New York on his first day in office to address a national engineering society and startled his audience with a wartime secret: just before the armistice, he had planned to drop an airborne army behind German lines, a full division carried in 1200 bombers and armed with 24,000 machine guns. He was sure it would have demoralized the enemy. The engineers gave him scant attention. In the world whose mechanical marvel was the Model T Ford, Mitchell's fantastic schemes of air war had a dreamlike quality. Only one newspaper mentioned his speech.

Mitchell found an unpleasant surprise awaiting him in Washington. The office of Military Aeronautics had been abolished by the army, and a new chief, the stern infantry hero, General Charles Menoher, became director of the Air Service. The ground officers were still in control. Mitchell made no complaint, but began work under Menoher as operations officer. He was a colonel once more, after reduction from his temporary wartime rank as brigadier general.

But there was no way to silence Mitchell. Washington heard little of General Menoher in the next few months. It was Mitchell whose name was constantly in the headlines. He had already begun the tireless campaign for American air power that was to end only with his death. Many of his veterans from France joined him, Tom Milling, Tooey Spaatz, Lewis Brereton, Chuck Chandler, Harold Hartney, Reed Chambers and Burdette Wright. These men trained and nurtured the tiny Air Service, while Mitchell fought to keep it alive.

He had been in office less than a week when Acting Navy Secretary Franklin D. Roosevelt invited Mitchell to testify before the Navy General Board, which was planning its air policy. This first session with the Navy was almost Mitchell's last, for he stunned the older admirals by predicting that planes would soon be freely attacking battleships. When Admiral Albert C. Winterhalter suggested that Mitchell's theory be tested, Billy urged that the Navy and the Air Service hold maneuvers so that planes and battleships could fight it out. Winterhalter agreed, but after the meeting, no more was heard of the plan. Mitchell was not asked to return, and each time he made a public claim for air power, the Navy made a more spirited defense of its battleships.

Mitchell began the almost daily flights around the country that were to take him more than 200,000 miles in the next four years, probably more than any other aviator of his day. He made speeches in most major U.S. cities on the promise of air power and commercial aviation; he inspected plane plants and airfields; he began appearing before Congressional committees; he consulted plane and dirigible manufacturers, inspected mail planes, flew regularly at Bolling Field to put his personal plane through its paces—and yet found time to win ribbons at horse shows, went fishing and trapshooting, and often took governmental officials for flights around Washington.

All the while Mitchell bombarded the perplexed Menoher with suggestions, some of them looking so far into the future as to leave Menoher speechless. Mitchell asked for long-range planes able to cross the Atlantic and return, two 900-foot aircraft carriers for the army, torpedoes and armor-piercing bombs, cannon and heavy machine guns mounted in his planes. Mitchell said that these were urgent needs of national defense, and he presented them as "emergency measures." All were ignored. Secretary of War Newton D. Baker and the General Staff thought Mitchell had lost his mind under the strain of war duty and that his ideas were beneath notice. One day Mitchell asked a headquarters officer what was being done with his suggestions.

"They're important to the country," Mitchell said. "And I haven't heard about a one of them." The officer laughed. "We're filing 'em," he said. There was a rumor that the War Department was filling a special cellar with Mitchell's proposals, known as "The Flying Trash Pile," but the flow of new ideas did not slacken.

A force of expert aviation mechanics must be trained, Mitchell insisted, with special pay and other privileges; major cities must have air raid protection, with alarms and plans for food rationing and medical care. Air transports must be built to carry infantry. Combined maneuvers of all services should be held to perfect defense against surprise air attack; commercial aviation should be expanded, if only to furnish a pilot reserve for war. He urged an all-metal bomber, a plan for an air shield of the Pacific coast, special plane-landing equipment, including skis. He also made a plea for a system of air routes to criss-cross the country.

Mitchell did not merely write memoranda. At McCook Field in Dayton his men experimented with new equipment—a variable pitch propeller for greater efficiency; parachutists developed techniques for airborne infantry, and dive bombers made pioneering experiments. Mitchell found a new chief of photography, George Goddard, who was soon making excellent high-level photographs from the air, including infra-red pictures taken by night. The Russian-born inventor, Major Alexander de Seversky, was working on a bombsight for Mitchell.

Only a handful of engineers, designers and test pilots knew how furiously Mitchell drove his men to develop the crude planes of the day, which were flown with almost no instruments. Mitchell pressed for an instrument panel—which he called "a cloud board"—to enable flight in bad

weather, with air speed indicators and inclinometers, so
that pilots could gauge their position. He demanded radio
systems, four-bladed propellers, a powerful radial engine,
better fuels, gliders, and control of battery fumes. He put
an end to the laborious hand-pumping of gasoline at airfields which wasted time and manpower. He constantly
studied inventions brought to his office—bomb sights and
wrenches, hydraulic transmissions, plane catapults, rain-
making schemes.

He was returned to his old rank of brigadier general
and also made Assistant Chief of the Air Service, but he
was still handicapped. There was so little money that the
airmen could not afford telegrams and were forced to com-
municate by mail.

Mitchell began to insist on a new kind of fighter plane,
one which was to revolutionize air combat and replace the
old canvas-covered biplanes held together by many rows of
wire. He called in a designer, Alfred Verville, and told
him to design a swift new racing plane—within ten days.

Verville was stunned. "What kind of a plane do you
have in mind, General?"

"I want you to design tomorrow's airplane. None of this
old stuff. I don't want a squirrel cage—no more wires and
struts and things protruding everywhere."

Verville worked day and night to produce Mitchell's
fighter—the first streamlined low-wing monoplane without
struts or bracing wires and with retractable landing gear.
Other engineers scoffed. "You shouldn't fool with Mitchell,"
one of them said, "He's crazy, and if you keep on with that
retractable landing gear, you'll ruin yourself. Who needs
retractable wheels? Suppose they forget to let 'em down
when they land?"

But when Mitchell saw the drawings of the plane he

shouted, "Now that's what I call an airplane! Exactly what we need. Why didn't you design this years ago?"

"General, you never asked me to," Verville said.

The plane was a sensation in the national air races of 1922 and won the event two years later. Verville said that Mitchell's prodding had brought the forerunner of fighter planes of the future. "In fact, it was the mother of the fighter types of World War II—including the Spitfire and the Zero."

While this work went on in secret, Billy kept up his vigorous campaign to convince the nation of the need for developing air power.

Franklin D. Roosevelt opened an attack on Mitchell for the Navy, saying that his views were "pernicious" and dangerous. Mitchell did not waver. He wrote his mother in the summer of 1919, "If I can get this on a firm basis within the next ten years, I shall consider my work pretty well done for the country."

But Hap Arnold, who came to Washington from his western post about this time, detected "angry impatience" in Mitchell, and took it as a sign that Billy was ready to defy army discipline in his effort to convince his opponents. Arnold warned Mitchell that the country failed to appreciate aviation because of ignorance—the plane was too young to be fully understood. But Mitchell thought resistance to his ideas came from a Washington conspiracy. "It's mostly the Navy," he said. "But it's old-fashioned generals, too."

Mitchell tried new schemes to dramatize air power—a patrol of the Mexican border to prevent illegal immigrants from swimming the Rio Grande; a pioneer flight of 9000 miles to Alaska and back by a group of army pilots; a cross-country race from New York to California, in which many old planes crashed and nine men were killed, and only ten fliers made the trans-continental flight. These feeble efforts founded United States commercial aviation and convinced a few officers that control of the air was essential to national security—but left the Army and Navy command unmoved.

Mitchell infuriated the Navy by announcing that his bombers could "make navies useless on the surface of the water." Secretary of War Baker scolded Mitchell and apologized to the Navy.

This episode spurred Mitchell to fresh attacks on conservative admirals. He told Congress that an "almost worthless" battleship cost as much as a thousand bombers and that a few of his planes could destroy the most powerful fleet. He alarmed congressmen with his charts and diagrams of a future air attack on the United States, in which the defending fleet was destroyed. Newspaper headlines followed: "America Helpless in Air War." Billy now found an ally in the veteran officer, Admiral William S. Sims, who said flatly that the day of the battleship was over and scoffed at more conservative admirals. "Can it be that the Navy is reluctant to give up the big ships to live in?" he asked.

After more than a year of such clamor, the Navy at last agreed to a complete test of ships against aerial bombs and furnished the old German vessels for the experiment. Mitchell formed his Air Brigade and drilled it secretly at Langley Field, setting such a furious pace that the skilled pilot, Jimmy Doolittle, who volunteered for Mitchell's staff, quickly left for the quieter life of test pilot. "I was Mitchell's aide for one day," he remembered later, "and on that one day, I moved faster and covered more country than I ever have before or since. He was a veritable dynamo of energy. Everything he did, he did just as hard as he could."

As the training went on, the Army and Navy combined to harass Mitchell. The Army ordered him to make no public statements about anything—especially about the Navy. In a public speech, Franklin D. Roosevelt said that planes would never endanger battleships. Admiral William A. Moffett, the Navy's air chief, said Mitchell was a meddler and a liar. Even General Menoher, Mitchell's superior, joined the attack and asked that Billy be fired: "He has given serious offense to the Navy Department by his public utterances and publicity . . . the effect of his activities has been so demoralizing to the personnel that he is a positive detriment." There was a furor when word of this reached the public. The country supported Mitchell overwhelmingly, and the new Secretary of War, John W. Weeks, gave Billy a mild reprimand and kept him in office.

A newspaper correspondent who went to sea with the fleet on maneuvers about this time reported to Mitchell, "You are throwing the Navy into convulsions. The entire fleet trembles with rage at the mention of your name."

Meanwhile, the bombing tests were held off the Virginia coast and Mitchell's planes sank the old German ships one by one, despite regulations which hampered them; Mitchell charged that the Navy was under orders to see that the Air Service did not sink the larger ships.

But it was soon over, the huge *Ostfriesland* went down in the climax of the test, and the nation saw that Mitchell had been right. The plane was the supreme modern weapon.

The sinking of the *Ostfriesland* made Mitchell a hero to aviators of the world and a figure of folklore in the United States, but when the Army and Navy agreed in their reports that the battleship was "still the backbone of the fleet," he had to risk insubordination to make clear the real meaning of the bombing tests. He defied orders to publish his report, which said that national defense must be revised at once, under a Secretary of Defense. He said that new danger faced the United States: "The problem of the destruction of seacraft by air forces has been solved and is finished. It is now necessary to provide an air organization and a method of defending not only our coast cities but our interior cities against the attack of hostile air forces."

General Menoher was shocked and opposed Mitchell's report so firmly that Billy submitted his resignation, saying that he was only a "source of irritation." Secretary Weeks still feared to dismiss the national hero and accepted a resignation from Menoher instead. Army pilots everywhere expected Mitchell to be made the new chief, but the President named Billy's wartime superior, General Mason Patrick, to head the Air Service once more. Eddie Rickenbacker commented, "General Patrick is a capable soldier but he knows nothing of the Air Service. His appointment is as sensible as making General Pershing Admiral of the Swiss Navy."

Patrick was growing old and he still had never flown, but he directed the Air Service with a firm hand. He told Mitchell, "I propose to be Chief in fact as well as in name. . . . I'll be glad to consult with you on all matters. But I want it understood—you'll give no orders. The final decisions will be mine." He had Mitchell make a written reply to his memorandum, setting forth the new rules.

Patrick soon became devoted to the cause of air power as he understood it, and though Mitchell was far from happy under him, he agreed to the terms and continued in office, determined to press his campaign. Patrick wrote of Billy, "Mitchell is very likeable and has ability; his ego is highly developed and he has undoubted love for the limelight, a desire to be in the public eye. He is forceful, aggressive, spectacular. He has a better knowledge of the tactics of air fighting than any man in this country."

The first clash between Patrick and Mitchell came when Billy's own report on the bombing tests mysteriously found its way into the newspapers. Patrick demanded an exact count of the copies of the report and had them traced, but Mitchell protested that it had been seen by hundreds of men at Langley Field and that he could not be blamed. Congress asked Secretary Weeks for a copy of this report and was refused: "I have been directed by the President to say that he considers the transmission of this report incompatible with the public interest." Mitchell's opinions on air power had now become unacceptable to official Washington. The views of the admirals and conservative infantry officers seemed as powerful as if they had been written into law.

The Army's harassment of Mitchell now became more intense than ever. At the end of 1921, just as Billy was to leave on a tour of inspection of air forces and aviation plants in Europe, Secretary Weeks got a report that Mitchell was mentally unstable and should not be allowed to leave. Weeks ordered Billy examined by Army psychiatrists; the doctors found him to be completely sane.

Mitchell could recall exactly dates and details of events from his early career; he rattled off long and complex information about aviation in all of its phases, ranging from the duties of flight surgeons to the qualifications of fighter pilots. He was not depressed nor elated, and though he said he was often worried over his problems he had trained himself to control his emotions and continue his work.

One doctor said, "He believes that he has done much toward the advancement of aviation and that he is one of the few whose foresight and aggressiveness have made possible a great future for the Army Air Service. Considering the officer's presumable ability and his rapid advancement . . . such ideas are not inconsistent with the normal content of thought . . .

"The officer's conversation is free, relevant and coherent. There is no flight of ideas, no . . . disturbance of the train of thought . . . manner is calm and collected . . . no evidence of mental or physical disease. He is reported as fit for full military duty."

This was enough for Weeks. He ordered Mitchell to leave on his European inspection tour.

Mitchell spent the first three months of 1922 in a whirlwind tour of Europe's airbases and plane factories, setting a pace that almost exhausted his companions, Captain Clayton Bissell and the plane designer, Alfred Verville.

Air officers welcomed Mitchell to Paris as the hero of the Chesapeake bombing tests and kept him busy for two weeks as consultant to a conference of the French air force, discussing the wars of the future. Mitchell reported to Patrick that the French were still planning for static trench warfare—though he had tried to convince them that mobility and air power were the keys to national defense. He also noted the French state of mind. "France is in abject terror of a future military Germany." But he also saw promise of progress in French aviation, which had already developed high-altitude bombers, which he said the United States should build at once.

On the Mediterranean, Mitchell, Bissell and Verville inspected a crude French aircraft carrier at work and saw French planes bomb an old German warship. Billy was glad to see the gospel of air power spreading but was not impressed by these French developments. "We are way ahead of them in this stuff," he said, "because it is impossible for them to conduct it on the scale that we did."

In Rome the party was entertained by King Victor Emmanuel, who had Mitchell recount the story of the bombed warships and sat in fascination as he heard of the work of the American squadrons. Mitchell liked the Italians and admired their mechanical ability, but told Patrick that they were unlikely to build a great air force.

It was in Germany that Mitchell found the threat to future peace. His sharp eye seemed to miss nothing. "The military spirit of Germany is by no means crushed," he reported. "It could be seen in the attitude of all the boys on the streets of every town we visited, and these towns were full of boys who will attain their majorities within a few years. . . . At the first opportunity, Germany may ally herself to any nation that is willing to help her. . . . Some countries, such as Austria, are absolutely helpless for the future under present conditions . . . therefore, Austria will join under Germany at the first opportunity. A joining of all the Germanic people will give them 100 million population."

His impressions were strengthened when he reached Berlin and visited the German military headquarters, now shrunken under terms of the peace settlement. "What few officers are left . . . are working diligently in the War Department building. The models of all their old battleships

Lt. Mitchell, youngest army officer at 18, in the Spanish-American War, 1898 (third from right). *Courtesy of the Smithsonian Institution*

On spy mission in Manchuria, Oct. 16, 1911, the day before the revolution against the Manchurian regime. Capt. Mitchell seated second from right. War lord Chang Tso-Lin, his host, is seated at left. *Courtesy of the Library of Congress*

Mitchell and his loyal aide, Lt. Clayton Bissell, 1922; Bissell later helped direct court-martial defense. *Courtesy of General Bissell*

Major Mitchell, first U.S. officer under fire in World War I, in French trench at Verdun. *Courtesy of the Library of Congress*

Mitchell, about 1924, in a flying suit o his design, ready to test a new plane *Courtesy of the Smithsonian Institutio*

Mitchell and his chief—and often his adversary—General Mason M. Patrick, an engineer officer who took up flying in his 60s. *Courtesy of the National Archives*

Mitchell in a 1922 pursuit plane many other pilots considered too "hot," the Thomas Morse, *Courtesy of the United States Air Force*

Billy Mitchell, about 1924.

Mitchell and General John J. Pershing ready to greet America's Alaskan fliers after their pioneer flight, 1920. *Courtesy of the United States Air Force*

Three men who helped build U.S. air power: Adm. W. F. Fullam, Orville Wright and Mitchell. National Air Races, 1922. *Courtesy of the United States Air Force*

Mitchell and his staff of Air Service officers. Celebration of Bastille Day and anniversary of Second German Offensive, July 14, 1920. *Courtesy of the United States Air Force*

Mitchell in his favorite plane, the old DeHaviland "Osprey," as he watched the bombing of the battleships off the Virginia coast, 1921. *Courtesy of the Library of Congress*

General and Mrs. Mitchell arrive in Washington, 1925, where he testified before an aviation board, just before his court-martial. *Courtesy of the Library of Congress*

Mitchell under fire at his court-martial. On his right, his council, Rep.
Frank Reid of Illinois; at his left, Mrs. Mitchell. *Courtesy of the United
States Air Force*

Mitchell and his wife at home in the Virginia hunt country about 1927,
after his retirement from the Army. *Courtesy of the Library of Congress*

The old German battleship, *Ostfriesland*, under fire from Mitchell's bombers —a near miss. *Courtesy of the United States Air Force*

Going . . . *Courtesy of the United States Air Force*

Deck of the old USS *Alabama* after Mitchell's bombs hit her in tests, 1921. *Courtesy of the United States Air Force*

Mitchell's smoke screen hides the *Alabama* before attack. *Courtesy of the United States Air Force*

The USS *Virginia,* crushed by bombs from Mitchell's high-level planes, 1923. *Courtesy of the Smithsonian Institution, Photo by United States Army Air Service, 20th Photo Section*

Pearl Harbor during Mitchell's inspection, 1923, when he wrote the prophetic report warning that Japanese planes would attack here early one morning, about 7:30; it happened 17 years later. *Courtesy of the Library of Congress*

Wreckage of the Navy dirigible, *Shenandoah,* destroyed in a storm in Ohio, in 1925, with a loss of thirteen lives—an incident which led Mitchell to denounce the Navy as "almost treasonable" in its handling of aviation. This outburst led to his court-martial a few weeks later. *Courtesy of the United States Naval Photographic Center*

Mrs. Zachary Lansdowne, widow of the *Shenandoah* skipper, before the Mitchell court-martial. General Douglas MacArthur at right. *Courtesy of the Library of Congress*

Major General Robert L. Howze, the stern president of the Mitchell court. *Courtesy of the Library of Congress*

are in the halls. . . . The German mind is still militaristic."

Mitchell's party was entertained by leading German aviators, among them men who would become famous in World War II—Ernst Udet, Erhard Milch and Hermann Göring. Verville saw that the Germans, too, had made Mitchell a hero and had accepted his theories of air power.

Mitchell visited the German aircraft plants of Junkers and Dornier where he saw a huge four-engined monoplane with wings five feet thick, and experimental air-cooled and diesel engines. Dr. Hugo Junkers, who took Mitchell through his plant, said, "this place has never been gone over so carefully—not by anyone." The party also met a scientist who had developed a turbine which he predicted would supplant the gasoline engine, and talked of flying bombs and rockets of the future. Mitchell said, "He's right, fifteen or twenty years from now, we'll see that kind of engine, and those kinds of bombs." (It was then seventeen years before World War II broke out in Europe).

Mitchell reported to Patrick that the Air Service must keep in touch with Junkers and Dornier and watch their developments. "The Germans combine resourcefulness of design with practical ability to create aircraft which is second to none in the world," he warned.

In Holland, Mitchell met Anthony Fokker, who had built thousands of combat planes for Germany during the World War, after being rebuffed by England and France. He and Bissell flew in one of Fokker's new planes and Mitchell encouraged Fokker to come to America and open a plane plant. (When he did come soon afterward, Fokker built the first plane to cross the United States non-stop).

The tour ended in England, where Mitchell reviewed RAF cadets, dined with Winston Churchill and his wartime friend, General Hugh Trenchard, and watched air force maneuvers. He reported on English devices for night flying, and on aerial torpedoes. The British, he wrote Patrick, would make formidable foes in the air.

When he returned to Washington in March, 1922, Mitchell prepared a massive report on all they had seen—a work of several volumes that weighed more than ten pounds, full of drawings and photographs of planes, engines, airfields and factories. The report detailed the speed, weight, armament and fuel consumption of all warplanes of western Europe, a summary that would have done credit to a team of master spies. It ended with another of Mitchell's warnings:

"All the great nations have assigned definite missions to their air forces, to their armies, and to their navies. In the United States we have not done this, and at this time, if we should be attacked, no one can tell what the duties of these three arms are." The coastal defenses were divided between so many branches, he said, that "our hands would almost be tied in case we were attacked by a first-class power."

Congress never acted on this report, and General Patrick himself probably did not read it.

Soon after he returned home, Mitchell flew a racing plane to a new world speed record of almost 225 miles an hour, a mark soon broken by his own fliers. He still made public speeches almost constantly, and one Philadelphia newspaper reporter gave this vivid description of the pilot-hero on the lecture platform: "General Mitchell has speed written all over him. He talks, thinks and practices speed. His very person is streamlined in real-man fashion. Just short of six feet in height, weight about 180 pounds, looking about ten years younger than his actual age, the most competent and intrepid pilot in America is as trim and fit as a college halfback. . . . The most conspicuous officer in any armed branch of the government looked the part. His dark hair parted over a high brow, his strong stern face and compelling eye, his entire person had speed, intelligence and pride of race written all over it."

In these years Mitchell, almost alone in the United States, collected "spy reports" from American military attaches abroad, keeping a file of information from England and Japan, where large air forces were being built. From London, Mitchell learned that Japan had ordered many new European planes, was building aircraft carriers—and that British instructors were training Japanese pilots. Mitchell urged his own chief engineer to greater efforts. "You have got to watch this foreign development. The Japanese have got type 30 Nieuports, the Breguet . . . and the Farman bimotor for bombardment. These are very fine ships. . . . Now, you are the bird charged with fixing these programs. . . ."

From Tokyo he had a warning from one of his officers that the Japanese "are working their heads off" to build an air force, and were using Mitchell's own ideas. "The Japanese are trying to build planes and motors and I believe it will be only a question of time before they can turn out a decent number." This officer complained that the army allowed him so little money for his inspection work that he could no longer travel by train and was reduced to spying by means of clipping newspaper items on Japanese aviation.

Mitchell was still working in secret with the one-legged Russian inventor, Alexander de Seversky, who was now perfecting a new bombsight which made all others obsolete. Mitchell and de Seversky were frequently closeted at

Bolling Field, working over their mysterious project. Sometimes, when de Seversky sent in his drawings in a spidery Russian script, Mitchell was forced to take them to a Washington delicatessen proprietor, who translated the inscriptions about an invention he could not understand. Finally, de Seversky called Mitchell to McCook Field, Illinois, where he had mounted a small model of his bombsight in a hangar. With the aid of a simple computer the sight released tiny bombs to fall on ship models below.

Mitchell was like a child with a new toy. He climbed to the platform to act as bombardier and shouted at each hit, "That's the stuff, Seversky! Let's get it down to Langley and drop some live ones."

De Seversky long remembered this scene. "I have never seen anyone so boyishly excited, so enthusiastic. He . . . acted the role of bombardier, then the pilot; then he was on the floor maneuvering the 'battleship' to test the bombsight under every conceivable condition."

A few days later the sight was installed in a plane at Langley Field. When de Seversky found the nose of a Martin bomber too small, he enlarged the opening with a hatchet and a hacksaw, squeezed up into the plane and called to Mitchell, "You'll forgive me? I had to remove my wooden leg to get in at all."

"Don't let that bother you," Mitchell said. "If the sight works, we'll just amputate the right legs of all our bombardiers."

The two flew over an old shipwreck in Chesapeake Bay to test the sight and found it "100 per cent accurate." The Air Service soon bought the sight, which was the forerunner of American models of World War II. De Seversky gave Mitchell credit for pushing this development, goading the Russian until he had perfected the instrument's gyroscopes and devised an artificial horizon and other improvements. He found Billy insatiable. "As a result of the energy and foresight of this great man, Billy Mitchell, America today leads the world in instrument flying."

At this time Mitchell also worked with Dr. Sanford Moss, who developed a supercharger that enabled Air Service planes to fly to high altitudes for their bomb practice.

Both devices were tested in 1923 when the Navy, after long delays, gave Mitchell the old battleships *Virginia* and *New Jersey* for bombing experiments off Cape Hatteras, North Carolina. The planes bombed from 10,000 feet, higher than ever before, and the new sight proved so accurate that the *Virginia* was sunk in twenty-six minutes after hits by fourteen bombs. Even after these second tests, the Navy refused to admit that battleships were obsolete and insisted that modern warships, able to maneuver under their own power, would have driven off Mitchell's planes. Mitchell was depressed when a truthful report of the bombing was kept secret by an admiral, who said, "It's true, every bit of it, but we can't let this out, or it would ruin the Navy."

Once more, the public failed to learn the real significance of Mitchell's performance. As he told Hap Arnold sadly, "Air power doesn't seem to be getting anywhere. I'm getting tired of this endless fight for funds, of feuding with old admirals or some idiotic committee with an ax to grind."

He was also having more trouble with General Patrick, who wrote of Billy in his confidential reports at this time, "This officer is an exceptionally able one, enthusiastic, energetic and full of initiative. . . . He is fond of publicity, more or less indiscreet as to speech, and rather difficult to control as a subordinate. . . . His enthusiasm sometimes carries him away."

There seemed to be no way for Mitchell to awaken America to the promise of air power without challenging the iron discipline of an army which was determined not to hear him.

But he was now on the verge of a new experience which would provide one of the great contributions of his career —he was ordered to tour the Pacific and report on United States defenses and the threat of foreign powers in the area. Mitchell had fought for United States aviation for five hectic years without noticeable effect. He welcomed his new assignment to the Pacific as an opportunity to continue his fight. He did not seem to suspect that the Army's motive was only to get him out of Washington once more.

6

"THE JAPANESE ARE NOW BOILING OVER"

Mitchell began his tour of the Pacific in Hawaii, in December, 1923.

He went ashore at Honolulu to find a gay, sleepy peace-time Hawaii, its defenses commanded by General Charles Summerall, an aging infantryman who knew nothing of air power. Within a few hours Mitchell had found the weaknesses of the island: "Our defense is based on a land army, coast defense guns and battleships, all of which are uncoordinated. A modern boy fifteen years old, who knows about air power and had a simple military training in high school, could work out a better system."

Hawaii was still very remote from the United States. There was no plane service to the islands, and Mitchell astonished the public by predicting to a news reporter that there would soon be plane flights from California, which would take only twenty hours. General Summerall and his officers were blind to the military threat from the air, and when they held maneuvers for Mitchell, he saw that they shifted infantrymen over the Hawaiian hills as if they were chessmen, and fought roaring battles off the coast with big ships, but gave no thought to planes. Summerall was thunderstruck when he learned of the notes Mitchell had begun to write for his report. "The personnel, particularly the staff officers," Mitchell noted, "are not familiar with the larger problem—in the air." One day, Mitchell said confidently, Oahu would be attacked by planes, and ground maneuvers of the army were dangerous, "apt to lead to erroneous conclusions."

Mitchell went everywhere, visiting all the islands, testing the few old planes, poking through barracks, firing on rifle ranges, making speeches, taking squadrons aloft for training. He also made a preliminary report to Patrick. Hawaii's defenses were hopeless, he said. "There are only two little pursuit squadrons with twenty-three planes . . . these would be put out of business in one encounter." They had no machine guns, the fliers never shot at targets and were not trained for combat. "They are unable to ward off any decided attack." And Mitchell was becoming more positive that such an attack would come. "Air power will certainly control the Pacific," he wrote.

As he left Hawaii six weeks later, Mitchell was still testing his theories. To the dismay of other passengers, the pilots he had trained delivered a mock attack on his steamer as it bore him westward, diving very near the ship before pulling away in simulated bomb runs. He watched his fliers through binoculars until they circled over their landing—they must remain in formation until the last moment, to avoid being shot down by alert enemy fighters.

General Summerall stormed angrily when he read the report Mitchell had left behind, and wrote Patrick that Mitchell's findings were "superficial impressions and academic discussions," based on daydreams and unsound assumptions of enemy action. Patrick tried to calm the general in reply, saying that Mitchell was over-enthusiastic, but that his views might have value, ten or fifteen years in the future. Meanwhile, there was little to worry about.

Mitchell had already warned General Patrick that he would go far beyond the usual inspection: "I shall study the whole Pacific problem from both an offensive and a defensive standpoint. . . . It will comprise the problem of destroying the enemy's armed forces . . . their power to make war."

America would be forced to fight here, Mitchell said, and he would look for "a solution of the problem which will allow us to carry on an offensive campaign across the Pacific ocean." Patrick could not glimpse Mitchell's vision —that an entirely new kind of warfare would be waged in the vast area, that air power would shrink the distances, overcome all other arms, and dominate the theater. Mitchell, it seemed, was the only man who saw, far in advance, the outline of World War II.

Mitchell sailed on to Guam, working night and day, poring over charts of the Pacific. He sent to Washington reports on islands Patrick had never heard of. Wake Island, though it was dismissed in atlases as a tiny brush-covered islet, should be used as an airbase or radio station—it was near the Marshall Islands, one of many chains through which the Japanese were developing air routes. He measured distances and spotted important points, all to become familiar in World War II—Midway and Guam and Truk, the Bismarcks and the Caroline Islands. Mitchell was the first airman to study the Pacific, and he was already revising previous strategic concepts for the area. He was writing a dramatic version of a Japanese attack on Pearl Harbor complete even as to the time of day, but the men for whom he was writing lacked the experience to enable them to grasp the meaning of his grim scenario of the future.

He stopped in Guam for a day or two, and reported that the garrison of 650 Marines was much too small, and that the "little dab" of air power—mostly antiquated seaplanes—should be strengthened or removed. He saw Guam as "a dominant factor in the military future of the western Pacific," and urged that the United States cling to it.

In the Philippines, Mitchell saw his old friend General Douglas MacArthur, who was, like General Summerall, blind to the use of air power in defending his islands. There was one pursuit squadron, whose few planes had come only three months earlier; the pilots were untrained. There was no system of command or operations. A so-called "air-group" had three officers and twenty-seven enlisted men, all of them doing office work. An observation squadron based on Corregidor had only five old flying boats—and Mitchell found that they were so underpowered that he could force one to rise from the water only in calm weather.

Mitchell reported to Patrick as gloomily as he had from Hawaii. The Philippines were guarded by a garrison of 12,000 troops, but 10,000 of these were natives whose language, backgrounds and customs were unknown to their American officers. He warned that the Japanese were keeping watch on the islands—they had an airway only twenty miles from Luzon, "within striking distance of Manila Field, Cavite Naval Base . . . Corregidor," all places where Japanese planes would attack one day.

Mitchell sailed on through Java and Singapore, still reporting to Patrick—the Dutch in Java would be stout allies, but their islands were open to Japanese assault. Singapore's defenses were weak, and Japanese farmers were on the very edge of the fortress. He went to India and hunted tigers, but found time to report on the strength of the Indian army, and sent charts of troop locations, airfields, military depots and shops.

He went into China, his first visit in thirteen years, and this time found it the most remarkable nation of the Pacific basin. He saw far into the future: "The Chinese themselves are extremely virile, democratic, industrious and very strong physically. Biologically they are undoubtedly superior to any people living. They are extremely intelligent and capable of carrying out any development that is desired." He told Patrick that though China was then being preyed upon by other nations, and had weak leadership, her potential was enormous.

Mitchell's real goal was a tour of Japan, which was then being swept by waves of anti-American sentiment. United States officers tried to stop Mitchell's visit at the last moment, and Patrick sent him a cable:

STATE DEPARTMENT ADVISES YOUR PRESENCE AT THIS TIME IN JAPAN LIABLE TO MISCONSTRUCTION BY JAPANESE STOP DO NOT ATTEMPT TO VISIT UNTIL WAR DEPARTMENT ADVISES.

But Mitchell could not be halted by nervous diplomats. After an exchange of cables, he was allowed to enter Japan as a tourist and pass through the country to catch a ship for home. He saw more in his brief trip than Americans working from the embassy in Tokyo had seen in years. He was soon telling Patrick that Japan would bear watching.

Spies, he said, were everywhere, and their calling was a most honorable one in Japan. Secret agents were placed in the service of foreign governments and allowed to work their way to positions of trust for many years. "The most elaborate system of espionage is maintained by them, especially within the United States." He also reported frankly on the hostility he saw on the streets. "The Japanese are now boiling over in anti-American agitation in their press. . . . Its object is to see if America will be 'scared.' "

Mitchell predicted that Japan, desperately seeking allies, would one day join with Germany. He saw Japanese cities growing rapidly, drawing people from the countryside to work in new factories—and many of these, never previously reported, were aircraft plants.

"Her military effort is now centered on her air force," he reported. "Already this new air arm is rapidly approaching the second in size in the world. . . . She now has many more men, more machines and more factories working on her air force, yes three times over, than has the United States." This effort, he told Patrick, was clothed in greater secrecy than Japan's stealthy preparations for her war with Russia a few years earlier, and this explained why American diplomats had not reported it.

Mitchell sent a list of seventeen factories which, he said, were rapidly producing planes, engines, bombs, torpedoes, military cars, and trucks. Mitchell thought that Japan, having seen the limitations of fleets of battleships, had turned to the air to become strong. He warned Washington, "Japan knows what a tremendous change is coming in the conducting of overseas operations. Naval systems of the past will give way to the air systems of the future. She is ready from a naval standpoint but is afraid of the air." It was a prediction that no diplomat and no other high-ranking United States Army Officer could have made.

Mitchell also warned Patrick that American prejudices

against the Japanese were dangerous, and helped to obscure the truth about their aviation. "One hears it often said that the Japanese cannot fly. Nothing is more fallacious than this. They can fly, are going to fly, and may end up by developing the greatest air power in the world. . . . It takes no longer to teach Japanese than it does Anglo-Saxons."

The Japanese, he said, were buying the best planes and equipment in Europe and copying them in their plants. "I believe there is no doubt that they have a striking force of at least 600 airplanes."

Just as he left Japan, from the harbor at Nagasaki, he had a close look at its growing power. The battle fleet, ready for maneuvers, was going to sea in the foggy morning—battleships, cruisers, eighteen destroyers and a fleet of submarines. "The first intimation we had that the craft were moving out was the coming of two squadrons of Sopwith pursuit planes from the airdrome of Sasebo. These were followed by several observation planes. Then submarines moved out, followed by the destroyers, light cruisers, battle cruisers, battleships and supply vessels. The whole thing struck me as being very well executed and smoothly done." Some of these ships were to play roles in World War II, and one of them would accompany the striking force against Pearl Harbor on December 7, 1941.

Mitchell sailed for home, once more busy on shipboard, this time writing the masterpiece of his career—a long, thorough study of the Pacific basin and its military future in the age of air power. He went home confident that he could make Army officials listen to his warnings, and that the United States would prepare before it was too late.

A WARNING UNHEEDED

The War Department received Mitchell's Pacific report with all the enthusiasm of a green demolition team handling an unexploded bomb.

General Patrick could not believe his eyes when he saw the first few pages, which forecast a war between Americans and Asiatics for control of the region. "This report is being studied, but due to the necessity of consideration of other matters, a reply will be delayed." He was to delay more than a year before giving his opinion—and it was to be two years before the Secretary of War saw the radical document.

All divisions of the Army were asked to comment on the report. War Plans said, "Many of the opinions expressed . . . are based upon the author's exaggerated ideas of the powers and importance of air power, and are therefore unsound. . . . None of these so-called conclusions are new; all of them have been advanced by General Mitchell before. . . . Since he so notoriously overestimates what could be done with air power by the United States, it is not improbable that he has likewise grossly overestimated what Japan could do and would be able to accomplish with air power."

General Harry A. Smith, Assistant Chief of Staff, who signed the War Plans comments, wrote, "While General Mitchell's report purports to be a report upon his trip to the Pacific Ocean, it in reality covers a much broader field. The document has been used . . . as a vehicle for propaganda for a unified and separate Air Service. . . ."

The Operations Division was even harsher. "The report is so voluminous, and contains so many statements which indicate a misconception of the true role and proper employment of air units . . . and such an exaggerated idea of the powers of aviation . . . that detailed comment on this report is believed to be unnecessary." Operations said that plans for war in the Pacific were being fully and constantly studied, and that aviation was being developed as rapidly as possible. (The United States had about sixty combat-ready planes at the time.)

Operations did agree that some of Mitchell's suggestions had merit—the authority of Army and Navy commanders in the Pacific should be clearly defined and some means of joint operations devised. United States cities should be guarded against air attack. Otherwise, Operations found little to approve.

The Intelligence Division said that Mitchell's report did not agree with its own, and that his estimate of the rate of aircraft production in Japan did not seem "to be borne out by the facts." The division had only scorn for Mitchell's hasty inspection: "The members of the U.S. embassy at Tokyo have the opportunities for inspection and contact never accorded General Mitchell in his hasty tour of the Far East. . . . It is understood that General Mitchell made no inspections of air stations in Japan and it is not understood how he could have carefully checked the information of his reliable sources."

The Japanese air force, by Intelligence estimates, ranked fifth in the world, and not second, and Mitchell's estimate that it had six hundred planes was "a grossly erratic conclusion." Forty years later Japanese military officials were to concede that Mitchell had been right in this count. Some of the Intelligence comments were trifling indeed: Mitchell had said that an aircraft plant at Kobe had 1200 employees, producing eighteen engines per month, and Intelligence corrected him—there were only 1000 employees, and production was twenty engines monthly. The division agreed that bicycle plants were making plane wheels, a musical instrument factory made screws for planes, textile plants produced fabric for covering fuselages and wings, but it saw no menace in these developments.

Even the Personnel Division attacked the report: "only a recitation of the aspiration of the Air Service rather than a description of actualities . . . will not bear careful analysis." As to Mitchell's prediction of a Japanese attack on Pearl Harbor, "It gives an interesting description of an attack on Oahu from the air which can hardly be considered more than a possible employment of the Air Service in a raid."

The Supply Division said Mitchell's views and recommendations were "imaginative," and that "none of these can be seriously considered for a moment . . . even were the War Department carried away as is General Mitchell."

And when he finally did comment, General Patrick found the report faulty in many respects. A Japanese strike at Pearl Harbor, for instance, "would not seem to be possible of execution at the present time." Mitchell had greatly overestimated Japan's ability to make war, since she lacked oil, steel, and other resources. Further, many of the United States shortcomings noted by Mitchell had been improved, but since there was no money to provide the Pacific air defense Mitchell proposed, little more could be done.

Thus one of Mitchell's most important contributions was cast aside, filed by the Army and forgotten. Though he was the first trained airman to study the area and its military problems, and he was the most insistent prophet of the inevitable clash between Japan and the United States —and of a vast war in the air—the Army's groundlings were deaf, dumb and blind to his warnings.

There were logical reasons for the Army's rejection, but the intense Mitchell lacked the patience to appreciate them—commanders with niggardly budgets could hardly maintain their tiny operations from day to day, let alone face the potential threat of air war. Mitchell had not troubled to suggest that it would take many years of slow, patient building to provide the security of the air force of his dreams.

The graphic details of Mitchell's work, not to be made public until 1967, were responsible for the War Department's reaction. Deep within the 323 pages of the report was buried a glimpse of the opening moments of World War II in the Pacific:

"Japan knows full well that the United States will probably enter the next war with the methods and weapons of the former war, and will, therefore, offer the enticing morsel which all nations that follow that system have done before.

"Japan also knows full well that the defense of the Hawaiian group is based on the island of Oahu and not on the defense of the whole group."

Then Mitchell described a scene he thought would inevitably be played out—the coming of a Japanese attack on Pearl Harbor:

"I believe, therefore, that should Japan decide upon the reduction or seizure of the Hawaiian Islands the following procedure would be adopted. Ten submarines would be loaded with six pursuit airplanes each. . . . Two airplane transports would be provided, each loaded with 50 bombardment planes. These ships could be equipped with a flying-off deck. . . . These seacraft would be started so as to arrive at the islands of Niihau in Hawaii and Midway, respectively on 'D' day. . . .

"As soon as set up and tested, those ships would fly to Niihau and then be ready to attack Oahu immediately. . . .

"The first attack would be arranged as follows: the Japanese pursuit, 60 ships organized into one group with three squadrons of 20 ships each; two squadrons to participate in combined attack with bombardment and one squadron remaining in reserve on alert. . . .

"The Japanese bombardment, 100 ships organized into four squadrons of 25 ships each. The objectives for attack are 1) Ford Island [in the middle of Pearl Harbor], airdrome, hangars, storehouses, and ammunition dumps; 2) Navy fuel oil tanks; 3) water supply of Honolulu; 4) water supply of Schofield; 5) Schofield Barracks airdrome and troop establishments; 6) naval submarine station; 7) city and wharves of Honolulu.

"No attention will be paid to the naval dry dock because it can be used only for docking and repair of vessels.

It is easier to sink these vessels than take time to destroy concrete work of dry dock . . .

"Attack will be launched as follows: bombardment, attack to be made on Ford Island at 7:30 A.M. . . . Group to move in column of flights in V. Each ship will drop . . . projectiles on the targets . . .

"I have gone into attack by an enemy in some detail to show how easily it can be done by a determined and resourceful enemy. . . . Actually nothing can stop it except air power. . . .

"I have put in a landing on Midway to show that it can be done. . . ."

He added, as if he expected staff officers in Washington to take him seriously, "Well may it be said, 'This sounds well, but what will our air force be doing in the meantime?' As things stand it would be almost useless. There are only two little squadrons of pursuit aviation and a total of 23 Thomas Morse airplanes. . . . A little dab of pursuit such as this is even worse than if none at all were here, because it gives an impression to those unfamiliar with aviation that some offensive power can be exerted by these few airplanes. . . ."

He expanded what he had told Patrick and Summerall about Hawaiian defenses—too few planes, no bombing equipment, no machine guns, no reserve of pilots or supplies, no intelligence or reconnaissance systems, no airways, no control of anti-aircraft. As he summed it up:

"In proportion to the strength and ability of the United States, the . . . air forces in Hawaii were by far the poorest I inspected in any country. As the safety of the Hawaiian Islands depends primarily upon air protection, this is an important matter."

The attack on Pearl Harbor happened almost precisely as Mitchell had predicted—seventeen years in advance.

Billy did not stop there. He wrote the same kind of plan for an attack on the Philippines, saying that bombers and fighters would strike Clark Field—as they were to do in 1941; that they would establish bases nearby, then reduce the garrison at Corregidor—from which General MacArthur was to escape to safety by submarine before his men surrendered. To guard against such attacks, Mitchell said, the United States should strengthen its air forces throughout the Pacific, and coordinate the efforts of Army, Navy and air officers. He said that a fleet of 650 planes, based on Hawaii, could prevent an attack there, under alert commanders.

He also wrote at length of how the war could be carried to Japan, what cities should be bombed, what warships hit, how to train men for night fighting, sea rescue work— he discussed even pamphlets of instruction.

Behind these defense plans were his theories of the coming struggle. A racial clash, yellow vs. white, was sure to come.

"The policy of the United States," he said, "in fact of all white countries having their shores washed by the waters of the Pacific Ocean, is to keep their soil and their institutions free from the ownership, the domain and the customs of the Orientals who people the shores of this greatest of all oceans.

"Eventually in their search for existence the white and

yellow races will be brought into armed conflict to determine which shall prevail."

Japan, as the leader of the Orient, was making careful plans. "She knows that war is coming some day with the United States, and it will be a contest for her very existence. The United States must not render herself completely defenseless by on the one hand thinking that a war with Japan is an impossibility, and on the other by sticking to methods and means of making war as obsolete as the bow and arrow."

Japan was also demanding an equal voice in world affairs, and was outraged by American policies toward her people. "The rumblings of this coming strife have ceased to be audible whispers, but are the loud protests of the Japanese people, the vanguard of the Asiatic, over the exclusion laws, the land laws, and the unequal treatment at the hands of our citizens. . . . Sooner or later the diplomatic means of handling these questions will fail and a physical means of impressing our will on a hostile state will be the only recourse. In other words, war."

This war, Japan realized, would come when both the United States and Japan developed large military forces in the Pacific. "Therefore sooner or later they must fight. The only question is how and when and where."

With the Army's rejection of this report, Mitchell realized that he must find other ways to arouse the American people to the dangers of future wars.

8

"GENERAL MITCHELL ... HAS BEEN SO LAWLESS"

Mitchell began the sixth year of his struggle for air power with a new sense of urgency, as if he could hear the bomb blasts on Pearl Harbor. It was 1924, his last year in uniform, and the nation seemed to be interested in anything but its defenses. Calvin Coolidge was running for President on a platform of economy—the income tax was slashed by 25 per cent, and in four years government spending had been cut in half. Mitchell knew that the President, the Secretaries of War and Navy, the Army General Staff and the Navy's General Board still fiercely opposed a unified air force and almost anything else he sponsored.

General Patrick, who had tried to persuade the Army to improve aviation by gentler methods than Mitchell used, confessed failure. "The Air Service is practically demobilized and unable to play its part in any national emergency, or even to meet the many peacetime demands for service." The Army soon afterward responded by cutting air strength even further, almost eliminating one group. Two squadrons were abolished and a surviving one, the 60th, was reduced to forty-two men. Patrick was quieted, but Mitchell merely attacked the harder.

Without knowledge of Secretary Weeks, Billy got the approval of President Coolidge to write articles on aviation for *The Saturday Evening Post,* his first appearance in print since Weeks had muzzled him in 1921 after the leak of his bombing test report. The new articles created a sensation. The first of them gave the public a glimpse of unrestricted aerial warfare of the future, when fleets of hundreds of planes would devastate entire nations so completely that they could not rebuild in wartime. "In a trice, aircraft have set aside all ideas of frontiers. The whole country now becomes the frontier, and one place is just as exposed to attack as another." He defended this kind of war as less expensive and more humane than past wars, since it would be briefer.

Mitchell conceded that wars must still be won finally on the ground, but he branded orthodox Army and Navy leaders as "psychologically unfit" to handle the decisive weapon, air power. He repeated his demand for a single unified air force, and insisted that commercial and military aviation would become dominant factors in the world.

Secretary Weeks seethed with anger. But Mitchell had only begun. The Navy had conducted half-hearted tests on a scrapped battleship hull by dropping sand-filled dummy bombs on its deck and exploding underwater charges nearby. The ship was sinking from the underwater explosions when the Navy turned guns on her and sent her to the bottom. Naval officers announced that the ship had withstood bombing and was sunk only by gunfire from other warships. Mitchell had observed these secret tests and was spoiling to expose the Navy's false claims. He got his chance before a Congressional Committee, and said, "no bombs were used in any shape, form or fashion." The Navy had used subterfuge, he said, and should be investigated.

Representative Frank Reid, a friendly Congressman from Illinois, drew many other striking comments from Mitchell: "The Army and the Navy, the oldest institutions we have, place everything on precedent. You can't do that in the air business. You've got to look ahead.

"I think if we plunged into war tomorrow it would take us at least two years to get on a par with England or Japan . . . an air force could reduce our Philippine islands easily and we couldn't defend them with our present armament."

Reid asked, "You say Japan could take the Philippines and Hawaii and we couldn't stop it?"

"Of course," Mitchell said.

Mitchell now began to make regular appearances before committees of Congress, always as a star witness quoted at length by newspapers. He grew bolder in his testimony, as if daring someone to challenge him.

Hap Arnold, the future Air Force chief of World War II, who was now stationed in Washington, sought out Mitchell in his office, the only one of its kind. He found Mitchell wearing golf knickers, with his feet on a big desk littered with sample plane parts, photographs, charts, and a fragment of a 2000-pound bomb. Model planes hung from the ceiling, twirling overhead. The walls were covered with pictures and souvenirs—the steering wheel of a Zeppelin shot down in France, diagrams of air attacks, water colors of fighter planes, the brass name plate of the old U.S.S. *Alabama.* There was a huge grinning tiger skull, the largest man-eater ever killed in Siam, Mitchell said. On his desk was a black book marked "Secret" listing the numbers and location of every Army plane, the only readiness record of its kind in the country. The book was pathetically thin.

Arnold tried to caution his old friend. "Billy, take it easy. We need you. Don't throw away everything just to beat out some guy who doesn't understand. Air power is coming."

Mitchell only smiled. "When senior officers won't see the facts you've got to do something, perhaps an explosion."

Arnold warned him to handle older officers more gently. "Stop saying all these things about the independent air arm that are driving these old Army and Navy people crazy!"

Mitchell was silent for a moment and then said, "I'm doing it for the good of the air force, for the future air force, for the good of you fellows. I can afford to do it. You can't."

General Patrick wrote in Mitchell's service efficiency report for this summer: "He is impulsive and . . . frequently shows evidence of temper and a tendency to use measures unnecessarily harsh. His recommendations frequently fail to take into account conditions actually existing. . . . He is erratic and his opinions on many matters are frequently biased."

Patrick meant that there was simply no money to build the air force of Mitchell's dreams—and that Mitchell had given up hope of awakening the services to the danger without violating military discipline. He thought Billy was ready to rebel.

Mitchell soon bore him out. He made a new charge against his opponents: "All critics in the Army and Navy are being silenced by high-ranking officers, and air-minded officers are afraid to speak. Even worse, many senior officers have falsified evidence to confuse Congress." When he read headlines on these charges, Secretary Weeks called in General Patrick. "You know that Mitchell's appointment as Assistant Chief of the Air Service expires in March. Do you want him reappointed?"

"I do," Patrick said. "He's difficult, but he knows the air, and he works with me in a fairly satisfactory way."

Weeks was not convinced, but he said no more. For the first time, Mitchell's uncertain status had been formally discussed. He could be removed as Assistant Chief at the pleasure of Patrick, Weeks or Coolidge, and if removed, would lose his temporary rank of brigadier general and revert to colonel. Mitchell was keenly aware of this, but he attacked as vigorously as ever.

He told Congress that the United States had only nineteen planes "fit for war," that the Army had ignored his Pacific report, and had failed to support him in his struggle with the Navy. He added, "I fully expect to be punished for my statements here today."

Both Weeks and the Navy called for a full explanation of all Billy's charges, and Mitchell wrote long memoranda citing scores of instances in which officers had been intimidated and offering evidence that American planes were feeble, obsolete, and poorly armed. Patrick urged Weeks to keep Mitchell in office, saying that he was guilty of nothing worse than "poor judgment," but Weeks had made up his mind. Newspapers began printing gossip that Mitchell was to be demoted and a headline said:

"FOES MAY FORCE MITCHELL OUT."

The New York Times, not always friendly to Billy, published a strong editorial in his defense: "It may be that General Mitchell sometimes talks indiscreetly but he should have credit of his admirable work in France . . . and for demonstrating that Army aviators could sink battleships with bombs. General Mitchell has done more by example and initiative to advance military aviation than any other officer in either the Army or the Navy . . . to get rid of him by demotion or exile would be a scandalous misuse of authority."

Congress tried to save Mitchell with a joint resolution praising his efforts to reveal United States military weakness: ". . . we hereby compliment Brigadier General Mitchell and commend his position in this matter . . . and severely condemn the evident purpose of the national administration in its attempt to punish and discredit him. We believe in his courage and in his devotion to the nation."

It was too late. In early March, 1925, Weeks requested Coolidge to remove Mitchell from his post. The immediate reason, he said, was false testimony Billy had given to Congress. Instead of nineteen United States planes ready for war, Weeks said, there were 1592, almost 800 of these in storage. He did not add that most of these were left over from World War I, and that Mitchell thought them unsafe for any flight, let alone for combat. Weeks revealed his bitter feelings toward Mitchell in the final words of his report to the President:

"General Mitchell's whole course has been so lawless, so contrary to the building up of an efficient organization, so lacking in reasonable team work, so indicative of a personal desire for publicity at the expense of everyone with whom he is associated, that his actions render him unfit for a high administrative position.

"I write this with great regret because he is a gallant officer, with an excellent war record. But his record since the war has been such that he has forfeited the good opinion of those who are familiar with the facts and who desire to promote the best interest of national defense."

Coolidge agreed and announced Mitchell's demotion and banishment. He was ordered to a remote army post, Fort Sam Houston, near San Antonio, Texas, where there was almost no aviation—and where he could no longer cause trouble in Washington.

Mitchell gave a statement to newspapers saying that his demotion was a small matter, but that the future of national defense was vital. The reactionary forces of old-line infantry officers and naval officers had opposed progress since the war, he said. "Armies and navies are no longer capable of . . . putting into effect the complete military policy for a country. The voice of the air must be listened to in all councils with equal force." Once more he called for a Department of Defense, and pledged himself to keep up the fight for aviation.

Mitchell was honored by a round of farewell parties before he left for Texas. Once he made a brief speech. Looking back over twenty years of struggle to persuade the Army to adopt new methods, he commented wryly, "It was with the greatest difficulty that the Army was made to adopt the telephone, the telegraph, the automobile and the radio. When all the people were illuminating their homes with kerosene, the Army continued to use candles. When the people used gas the Army used kerosene, and when all else used electricity the Army continued for years to stick to the old illuminants.

"In the Indian campaigns the savages were better armed than our regular troops, as were the Spaniards in 1898,

and as our opponents would have been in the World War
had we not taken the weapons of our associates."

At one party, scores of officers said they were applying
for transfers to Texas, to go with him. They would resign
if this was refused. Mitchell was furious. "Sit down, every
darned one of you. This is insurrection. Not one of you
will resign. Not a one. And that's an order."

Then, as if the thought had not occurred to him before,
he said slowly, "Who will carry on . . . when I'm gone?"
There was a long silence. One of his officers remembered
years later, "We obeyed him. We obeyed him the rest of
our lives. And long after he was dead."

Even his old Navy adversary, the former Secretary, Josephus Daniels, mourned Mitchell's banishment and said he
would not have demoted him if he had been Secretary of
War. "I don't think we can adequately protect our coast-
line without the airplane," Daniels said. "The thing today
is the conquest of the air, and America is only playing
with the idea when it ought to be leading."

The press praised the deposed rebel as if he were dead.
The Cleveland *Press* said, "We may wait a hundred years
for another such display of courage."

It was soon clear that Mitchell could not be muzzled,
even in distant Texas. The magazine *Liberty* published
one of Billy's biting articles, "Exploding Disarmament
Bunk: Why Have Treaties About Battleships When Airplanes Can Destroy Them?" A new book, *Winged Defense,* appeared, based on his writings and testimony before Congress. Mitchell had not obtained permission to
write the book, and he invited the Army to make trouble:
"The truth of our deplorable situation is going to be put
before the American people, come what may. If the War

Department wants to start something, so much the better. . . . Then we will have a chance to remedy the unfortunate situation."

Billy was assigned pleasant quarters on the parade ground at Fort Sam Houston, but as Air Officer he had nothing to do. He was pursued by editors and publishers and often flew about the country. Once he flew to San Diego and gave a fiery speech, saying that United States air forces were "almost extinct," and that the country would learn its lesson, as usual, from "the disaster of war." He inspected some new Navy planes in San Diego, clumsy metal flying boats with which the Navy planned to make the first flight from California to Hawaii. When he discovered this, Mitchell studied the projected flight thoroughly.

He found that the Navy pilots, led by Commander John Rodgers, were not practiced navigators and had not made long over-water flights. The planes would be overloaded, carrying five men each, and must buck headwinds. They were to refuel from ships which lay in a picket line at 200-mile intervals. Mitchell was dubious about the plan. The real purpose of the flight, he thought, was to gain publicity for the Navy to counter the Army's success in a round-the-world flight directed by Mitchell. He left California with the feeling that the Navy's PN planes would not reach their goal.

This flight and the loss of the Navy dirigible *Shenandoah* in early September, 1925, stirred Mitchell to new indignation and led to the end of his military career.

The Pacific flight was plagued by bad luck from the start. Three planes tried for Hawaii, but one failed to take off because of its heavy load, another plopped into the sea just offshore, and the third, carrying Commander Rodgers and a crew of four, was in trouble. Within 300 miles of Hawaii it was running out of gas. The plane gave a distress signal and fell silent. Ships combed the area in vain, and the nation kept a long vigil for the downed fliers. While the search continued, a naval disaster was in the making in the skies over Ohio.

The large dirigible *Shenandoah,* the Navy's "battleship of the skies," had been ordered to the midwest during the season of autumn storms despite protests by her skipper, Commander Zachary Lansdowne. The big airship was to soar over state fairs of the region and impress the great crowds with the Navy's progress in aviation.

The *Shenandoah* flew west from Lakehurst, New Jersey, and by nightfall was over Pennsylvania, rising above the Alleghenies in a moonlit sky, its crew of forty-three watching small towns light up in the dusk below. The air was smooth and there was no hint of trouble. Most of the crew went to sleep early. The ship gave no sign of weakness from storm damage of some months before, when she had been ripped from her mooring mast. But she flew with most of her safety valves missing—ten out of eighteen valves had been removed by the crew for economy and convenience.

About midnight the ship's radio room heard a message that severe thunderstorms were raging over the Great Lakes, and the operator took the report to Lansdowne, who studied it without comment and went to his bunk. "Don't call me unless something unusual comes up," he said. Soon after 3 A.M., when lightning was flickering on either side of the ship, Lansdowne was called. The *Shenandoah* was rolling a little and lurching through headwinds at about 3000 feet.

The weather officer reported that storms were gathering all about them, and that only the south was open. Lansdowne shook his head. "That storm's still a long way off. I want to keep our course as long as we can." But by now, near Cambridge, Ohio, the ship was barely moving, even with engines at full speed. Two people in the darkness below looked up to see the huge ship sailing beneath a "boiling cloud" that looked as if "two storms had come together."

By 5 o'clock the engines began to misfire, and a few minutes later the crewman at the elevator controls shouted, "Captain, the ship's started to rise!" Lansdowne told him to check her, but the elevatorman fought the wheel in vain. The nose of the ship went down as she soared upward, waking all the crew. Her gas bags were now dangerously distended by pressure, at 97 per cent of capacity. Crewmen uncovered safety valves, and released some excess gas; the ship steadied a bit. The cook was awake by now, cursing the navigator as crockery crashed in his gallery. Taut wires snapped somewhere in the ship. Water lines were broken, the engines faltered. The ship was now 1200 feet above the safe pressure level, at 5000 feet, "swinging like a pendulum" as she rose into a dark cloud. She was entering the eye of a squall. Her rise halted at 6300 feet and the *Shenandoah* fell to 3200 feet in less than two minutes. Some gas bags had already burst, and hung flabbily.

Lansdowne attempted to turn her south at last, but she rose once more and two engines failed; there was a heavy vibration and a crash far forward. The ship began to come apart at 6200 feet. Girders and wires snapped, gasoline spewed through the interior, and the *Shenandoah* was torn into three parts. From below, several people watched the tail section float away, flapping tatters of torn fabric. The forward section, bearing most of the crew, plunged swiftly toward earth, but as the engines fell off, rose and drifted around open at both ends. Bodies began dropping below. The center section floated lightly to the ground, carrying four survivors.

The tail section struck trees as it came down, but fifteen of its men survived. The forward section drifted as high as 7000 feet before its men slashed gas cells and brought it down, with several survivors. Thirteen men were dead, Commander Lansdowne among them. Looters and souvenir hunters soon found the wreckage and carried away everything they could find. The Naval Academy class ring was wrenched from the finger of Lansdowne.

Criticism of the Navy was heard with the first news of the tragedy, and Secretary of the Navy Dwight Wilbur tried in vain to explain. In Texas, Billy Mitchell was deluged with requests for a statement from reporters in many parts of the country. He did not disappoint them. He dictated to his secretary a long, angry indictment of American military aviation and the old-fashioned officers who used it so badly. He called in reporters at 5 A.M. on September 5, gave them copies, and read parts of his charges:

"These accidents are the result of the incompetency, the criminal negligence, and the almost treasonable negligence of our national defense by the Navy and War Departments."

The loss of the *Shenandoah* puzzled him, he said—but an accident had weakened her structure, and a shortage of safety valves on her gas bags had been fatal. The trip had been used for Navy propaganda. "What business had the Navy over the mountains anyway?"

The loss of John Rodgers and his crew of the PN-9 in

the Pacific—they had not yet been rescued—had been caused by "primitive, good-for-nothing big lumbering flying boats." They had been overloaded, and refueling ships were too few.

Such accidents, Mitchell said, were caused by officers who were ignorant of aviation, who treated fliers as "pawns in their hands," and browbeat them when they complained. This conduct of aviation was "so disgusting as to make any self-respecting person ashamed of the cloth he wears.

"As a patriotic American citizen, I can stand by no longer and see these disgusting performances . . . at the expense of the lives of our people and the delusion of the American public.

"The bodies of my former companions in the air molder under the soil in America and Asia, Europe and Africa, many, yes, a great many, sent there directly by official stupidity. We may all make mistakes but the criminal mistakes made by armies and navies, whenever they have been allowed to handle aeronautics, show their incompetence. . . . This, then, is what I have to say on the subject, and I hope that every American will hear."

Mitchell's fierce attack made headlines across the country, and there was an angry reaction. Mitchell said he would welcome a court-martial if it would awaken Americans. As to the opinion of the Army and Navy about his statement, "They know that it's true. Know that every word is true. That's why it's going to sting."

Within less than a week of Mitchell's attack, President Coolidge appointed a board to investigate aviation, and Mitchell was ordered to appear before it in Washington. Already there were rumors that he was to be tried by an

Army court-martial for insubordination, and that the board hearing was merely to prepare the public for his conviction. Mitchell shipped eight hundred pounds of aviation documents to Washington and followed them by train. When a reporter asked, "Are you afraid to appear before the committee, General?" Mitchell replied, "Piffle." He was greeted in Washington by a crowd of about 10,000, and American Legion bands blared a welcome. The next day Billy rode in a parade down Pennsylvania Avenue and made a brief speech. His supporters carried placards along the streets proclaiming,

WE'RE FOR GENERAL MITCHELL
AMERICAN FIGHTER UNAFRAID

A few hours later the Army announced that Mitchell would be court-martialed soon after he appeared before the aviation committee, now called the Morrow Board.

Mitchell prepared for his trial by engaging Representative Frank Reid of Illinois as his lawyer, a tall, intelligent man with a keen wit and a sympathy for Mitchell's views. He had often befriended Billy in Congress. When the Army revealed that a dozen high-ranking generals would try Mitchell, Billy told reporters, "I demand to be tried by a court of flying officers. No man should sit in judgment on me who doesn't know flying. . . . Why, they're reverting to the medieval practice of coercion. It's like the old trials of heretics. Those charges have been so worded as to give me no chance to prove the truth. I think I'll insist on an open trial. The American people are interested in the truth."

Reid said that the Army and Navy were punishing Billy,

a faithful officer, for giving "timely and judicious advice on matters of great importance."

"Rome endured as long as there were Romans," he said. "America will endure as long as there are Mitchells."

9

"THIS AIN'T
A VAUDEVILLE SHOW"

Excitement grew in Washington as Mitchell's trial drew near. Newspapers were full of the case, and of pictures of Mitchell, his friends and his opponents. A national hero was being tried for heresy by his superiors, and the country watched in fascination. There were reports that the Army would hire a huge auditorium for the spectacle. Dwight Davis, the new Secretary of War, growled unhappily, "This is serious War Department business. It isn't a vaudeville show—or an advertising scheme."

The Army chose an old government warehouse near the Capitol as the site of the trial, a small, dark, unheated building with peeling paint and splintering floors which was hastily renovated. Few spectators could crowd their way into the place.

Mitchell and Reid planned their defense with the aid of many aviators and public officials who volunteered to serve. A dozen stenographers worked in Reid's office, and an endless stream of defense witnesses came, each to give his story in support of Mitchell. One of Billy's old friends, Captain Clayton Bissell, who acted as Reid's assistant, gathered the witnesses and organized their testimony. The group decided at once that Mitchell was guilty of insubordination as the Army charged, and that the trial could have but one purpose—to educate the American people to the need for national defense based on aviation.

Bissell knew how important public attention would be. "To convince the country, we must keep our story on the front pages of the newspapers every day," he said. "If we slip off for a day, we must find a way back. We'll need something spectacular, new stuff every day. It's going to be a job."

Other lawyers advised Mitchell to plead guilty, to save time and to make the issue of air power all the clearer. Reid refused. "Nothing doing. So long as I'm in the case he'll defend himself. If they'll let us prove that he's been telling the truth, and that he finally got to the point where nobody would listen to him, then we've got a chance."

Billy and Reid and Bissell and their volunteer helpers went to work, accumulating and sorting evidence. They spread Mitchell's long San Antonio statements on tables, cut them into sections, numbered each of Mitchell's charges, and assigned someone to find documents and witnesses to bolster each charge. From the hundreds of witnesses, Reid chose a few dozen whose testimony would be clearest and most telling. On October 27, when the task of sifting the stacks of documents was still incomplete, Mitchell was called to trial.

A great crowd that encircled the block before the Capitol watched the Mitchells arrive, the General immaculate in a new uniform with many ribbons on his chest, and Mrs. Mitchell in a black coat and hat. The couple waved cheerily to the applauding crowd and pushed to the inside. One reporter said that Mitchell looked "like a small boy on a picnic. If his nonchalance was insincere, then Mitchell's a great actor." Billy strode through the courtroom swinging his malacca cane and burst into the judges' chamber to shake hands with the generals who were to try him. A few minutes later he took his seat and the generals, now grim-faced, came to a long table in front of the crowded room. It was the highest-ranking court-martial ever assembled in the United States.

The president of the court was General Charles P. Summerall, whose Hawaiian defenses Mitchell had criticized so sharply. Mitchell had known many of the judges well for years, and one of them, General Douglas MacArthur, had been a boyhood friend. But none of them was a flier— all were infantrymen, cavalrymen, artillerymen or engineers.

The generals had hardly settled in their seats before Reid stunned the crowd with a bold attack on the court. "I challenge the right of General Albert L. Bowley to sit on this court."

General Summerall glared at the defense lawyer. "On what grounds, sir?"

"On the grounds of his prejudice, hostility and animosity to the accused."

Reid held up a newspaper clipping and read from a speech Bowley had made only a week before. " 'The changing of our whole system of national defense should not be attempted without careful and mature consideration. . . . Should we put it aside for the visionary proposition of a national Defense Department?. . .

" 'A single air service? Do we want this? The backbone of every army is the infantry . . . there is no more reason for a single air service than there is for a single medical corps. . . .' "

The generals filed into their anteroom to decide the question and left General Bowley sitting alone, facing newspaper photographers. When the court returned, Bowley was dismissed. The remaining generals gazed expectantly at Reid, who paused and said, "We wish to challenge the right of the president, General Summerall, to sit as a member of the court."

The crowd buzzed in surprise and Summerall chewed at his lips, his eyes blazing with indignation. Reid quoted Summerall's statements. " 'Aviation is a new arm. We all admire it. It is spectacular . . . but the public is being misled by fanciful and irresponsible talk emanating from a source . . . whose experience in war is limited to the very narrow field of aviation.' "

Reid then read from Mitchell's report of weak Hawaiian defenses under Summerall, defenses which "would lead to certain defeat in time of war." Summerall nervously rubbed his head as Reid told the court of shortages of planes, guns, radios, ammunition and other equipment on Hawaii, and of Army and Navy officers who refused to speak to each other, making cooperation "practically impossible." Reid also noted that Summerall's reply to Mitchell's criticisms had been to dismiss them as superficial, unfair and academic. The lawyer insisted that Summerall be dismissed from the court.

The general spoke, red-faced. He admitted making those statements and looked at Mitchell. "I had regarded his inspection as friendly. I had no personal prejudice toward him, although I thought his report was untrue, unfair—and ignorant."

A long "oooooh" came from the audience. Summerall

then dismissed himself. "In view of the bitter personal hostility toward me by Colonel Mitchell, I couldn't consent to sit, and I shall ask the court to excuse me." He retired and General Robert Howze, a grizzled Texas cavalryman, became president—"The best cavalryman who ever rode a horse," newspapers said.

Reporters who followed Summerall from the room found that he had a deep personal grudge against Mitchell. "I have kept an open mind on Mitchell's case. I took him into my home as a friend when he came to Honolulu. I placed a private car at his disposal. I loaned him an airplane. Only ten minutes before court convened I shook hands with him. Now it's all over. We're enemies, Mitchell and I."

Reid ousted one more officer, General Fred Sladen, the commandant of West Point, and the court was ready for the trial.

Reid made a long plea for dismissal of the case. The tall lawyer paced before the narrow table, his high-pitched voice reaching strongly throughout the room, black eyes glittering in a pale face, his long neck stretching now and then above his bow tie. Reporters thought he was more like a schoolteacher than a lawyer.

"I consider this the most august tribunal that has ever been called upon to act on any question since the Magna Carta," Reid said. "You have not only the rights of the individual here. You have the basis, the pillar of society here. . . . The trial of this case goes to whether or not the republican form of government can last without the public and without the public's opinion as the basis for action. . . ."

As to Mitchell, he had done no more than his duty in calling attention to weaknesses of the country's defense.

President Coolidge in a recent speech said that officers should give their views to public officials, "and that is the only offense charged, and the only offense for which he can be charged. Thank you."

The charges against Mitchell were fifty-two pages long, but they were read six times, until the generals were groggy. After three days of argument the army prosecutor, Colonel Sherman Moreland, said that Mitchell, like all others in uniform, gave up personal liberties such as free speech when he enlisted. This had to be, he said, or ". . . the Army of the United States would be left to rot on Government soil."

Reid scoffed. "If his argument is right, a military court is greater than God himself. . . . Are you going to invoke the old Spartan system? . . . If they didn't like a person . . . if they didn't like his looks, they would banish him. It's just the same idea as challenging a truthteller."

It was in vain. The court ruled that it had jurisdiction over Mitchell and that he must stand trial. Billy was ordered to stand and state his plea. He called out so loudly that spectators were startled, "Not guilty!" He replied in the same ringing voice to each of nine charges. Reid presented a list of seventy-one defense witnesses, and the trial finally began.

Reid opened by saying that he would prove Mitchell's charges were true, and that he had made his statement in San Antonio "in the hope that it would arouse the conscience of the American people, and that they would . . . through their representatives, cause the evils to be corrected." The major theme of the defense was, Reid said, "That Colonel Mitchell, after exhausting every usual means to safeguard the aerial defense of the United

States, without result, took the only way possible that would cause a study of the true conditions of the national defense to be made." Was he to be punished for trying to save his country, and penalized because of his vision?

One of the first witnesses was Major Carl "Tooey" Spaatz, a World War veteran who had shot down three German planes, and who was to become commander of United States Strategic Air Forces in World War II. Spaatz described the pathetically weak air service, with most of its 1800 planes obsolete, and half of its so-called "standard" planes left over from the war. Only fifty-nine planes in the United States were fit to fly, Spaatz said—and he could put fifteen fighter planes into the air only by pulling all his officers from their desks.

"Do you think aviation is being retarded by the War Department?" Reid asked.

The prosecution objected, but Spaatz was too quick. "I do," he shouted. The crowd applauded.

General Howze took over the grilling of Spaatz.

"Who is responsible for this?"

Spaatz nodded to General William Graves, who sat at Howze's elbow. "The commander of the Sixth Corps Area, sir." Graves said testily that he had never denied help to the air squadrons.

Spaatz replied that he had once tried to find a field for gunnery practice for his pilots, and that the Army not only did not help—but also refused to pay the annual rent on a field provided by the citizens of Oscoda, Michigan. "How much was that rental?" Reid asked. "One dollar a year," Spaatz said. The crowd's laughter drowned out the witness, and Howze hammered for order.

Many other pilots came to the witness stand, and as they

supported Mitchell stoutly, the court seemed to grow more hostile, especially General Graves, who often mumbled his complaints and acid comments so that they could be heard by spectators.

Major Hap Arnold appeared and challenged the claim of General Hugh Drum, who had insisted that United States air power was the equal of any in the world. The United States had eight pursuit squadrons, France had thirty, Italy twenty-two, and England thirteen. The prosecution claimed that the Atlantic and Pacific would protect the United States from attack, but Arnold insisted that planes had "annihilated" distance—and that since planes had flown the oceans, they could attack American cities.

The judges spoke crossly to Arnold. "Do you consider duty in the Air Service more dangerous than serving in the infantry, in wartime?" Arnold said that the airmen had 23 per cent replacements during the war, as against 7 per cent for the infantry, but the judges pressed him for actual figures of deaths. "We have data," Arnold said, "but every time we try to get something concrete, we find three or four sets of figures on casualties, as issued by the General Staff, and we don't know what to use." Arnold left the stand. He was soon to be "banished" from Washington and to spend many years in distant posts.

Another flier, W. G. Schauffler, said he was an air reserve officer.

"Did you ever have your squadrons together?" Reid asked him.

"Never. I never saw but two of the commanding officers, and those unofficially. They assembled the squadrons only once, for a parade."

One of the judges broke in. "What contact and influence do you have with the officers in your group?"

"I have none."

"Then why do you remain in the position you're in?"

"Lord knows. I don't!"

The judges asked Schauffler about his wartime flying, to probe Mitchell's claims that anti-aircraft fire was ineffective. "What altitude did you fly?"

"From treetop height up, about 500 feet."

"Under what orders?"

"Common sense."

"We were all in Europe, and I never saw a plane fly as low as 500 feet."

"You must have been in the dugout, sir."

Major Gerald Brandt, of the General Staff, was next to testify. Reid asked him about Mitchell's secret report on the Pacific.

"When did he make this report?"

"In October, 1924."

"When did this report reach you through channels?"

"Saturday."

"Do you mean last Saturday—here in October, 1925?"

"Yes, sir."

Brandt said the Army had told its officers that since the report contained Mitchell's own opinions, they should give it no consideration.

Brandt described recent Hawaiian maneuvers, in which the Navy refused to submit to a unified air command, so that orders had to pass through many officers of both services and were delivered too late. He also said the Air Service was deteriorating. "The best pilots are leaving and the flying fields built during the war are run-down."

Major Roycroft Walsh of the Air Service also tried to testify about the Hawaiian maneuvers, but the prosecution stopped him. The war games were secret and confidential, the Army lawyer said.

"How can they be?" Reid asked. "They were published

every day in Honolulu newspapers." Later he held up to the court a book published by a House Committee, hearings on the Hawaiian maneuvers that told all that Walsh had been forbidden to say. "Here is absolutely everything that was presented this morning," Reid said angrily, "published in these reports. Somebody ought to determine what is confidential!"

The war ace, Eddie Rickenbacker, took the stand and conceded that he had shot down twenty-six planes and balloons.

"How many hours were you in the air?"

"Approximately three hundred."

"How many hours over enemy lines?"

"Approximately three hundred."

"How many hours exposed to enemy anti-aircraft fire?"

"Approximately three hundred." He added that he was never hit, that the fire was ineffective. He said planes left over from the war should be scrapped. "It's dangerous to have them on hand. The graveyards at our flying fields show that." The prosecution moved to have his remark about graveyards stricken from the record.

Lieutenant Harold L. George, who was to become chief of the Air Transport Command in World War II, told of towing a target for anti-aircraft gunners who never scored a hit. "I towed it for about an hour and came down and asked how things were going. And the colonel who was running this anti-aircraft gun told me that he had quit long before. He said operating that gun was like trying to pat his head with one hand and rub his stomach with the other." The crowd broke into laughter.

The discipline of the court had sagged and laughter was now louder and more frequent. Even soldiers standing around the walls joined in. The judges strolled in late, nodding and speaking to Mitchell, lolling back in their chairs and yawning as witness after witness droned on. General Howze had at first sat very erect, calling out sternly after each ruling by the court lawyer, "There being no objection, under the Thirty-First Article of War the ruling of the law member is made the ruling of the court and shall so stand." Now Howze slumped in his seat, feet stretched far under the table, and mumbled, "Ruling of the Court."

Lack of control reached the point that Reid complained. "If the court please, there's so much noise in the room that I can't marshal my thoughts." Howze directed the soldiers to obtain order. A sergeant barked, "Don't go off so loud. This ain't a vaudeville show!"

One judge, General King, played with a rubber band, chewing on it, holding one end between his teeth and stretching it far in front of his face. Spectators watched intently. "If that band ever breaks," a newspaper said, "many will quit going to the trial."

Colonel O. C. Pierce, a personnel officer, took the stand and reported on pilot ratings. Only thirty men in service were rated as superior pilots, he said. He was asked to classify these by type.

"One attack, twenty-one pursuit, five bombardment, and one unclassified."

"What is the unclassified one?"

"He flies anything."

"What is his name? Have you got anybody in that list?"

"General Mitchell is the unclassified one."

Mrs. Zachary Lansdowne, the widow of the *Shenandoah* skipper, testified one day, a pretty young woman in black, who told the court that the Navy had tried to force her to make a false statement about the loss of the dirigible. Reid then read from her testimony before the Naval inquiry into the airship disaster:

" 'My husband was very much opposed to this flight and protested as vigorously as any officer is allowed to do to his superiors . . . no officer cares to earn the stigma of cowardice or insubordination.' "

Reid asked: "Did you give that testimony?"

"I did."

The court ruled that this testimony be excluded from the record. Reid shouted in vain that "it has been printed in every newspaper in the world."

Mrs. Lansdowne was allowed to tell how Captain Paul Foley, prosecutor of the *Shenandoah* inquiry, had tried to make her rehearse her statement to the court, and attempted to browbeat her.

"He told me that I had no right to say that the flight was a political flight, as the taxpayers in the Middle West had a perfect right to see their property, to which I answered that in the case of a battleship you wouldn't take it to the Great Lakes and interest the taxpayers in their property, to which he answered that it couldn't be done—and I said that it couldn't in the case of the *Shenandoah*, but they were so stupid it had to be proven to them." Movie cameras whirred as Mrs. Lansdowne left the stand. Her testimony made newspaper headlines, and the country was convinced of the Navy's guilt in attempting to conceal the facts of the *Shenandoah* tragedy. Many editorials called for the resignation of Secretary Wilbur.

Reid then called Earnest Sheehan, an Ohio newspaper reporter who had reached the wrecked *Shenandoah* within an hour of its crash. Survivors had talked freely with him, Sheehan said, until the arrival of a Commander Klein of the Navy. "He requested me not to write the cause of the wreck—what I had determined in my investigation. He asked me not to mix in it."

"You don't mean to say that Commander Klein intended you to permanently suppress any facts?"

"That was the impression I got."

When Sheehan said that the Navy had not called him or any eyewitnesses to its inquiry, he was quickly excused.

The next witness, the aging Admiral William S. Sims, caused a stir in court. He was a handsome, gray-haired Navy rebel, a staunch supporter of air power, with a quick mind and incisive voice. Reid asked, "What is the Navy's policy for handling aviation?"

"As I understand it, the Navy hasn't any defined policy. It is going along from day to day, more or less in a higgledy-piggledy way."

"Are Navy officers afraid to speak their convictions about aviation?"

"Yes. One man I know is as strong for air power as I am, but he refused to speak out before a group of officers who were talking aviation. When I asked him why, he told me, 'I can look around this group and see half a dozen men who would beat me at the next selection for promotion, and I've got a wife and two children.' That's the trouble," Sims said.

He added that the men then leading the Navy were poorly prepared for their roles:

"Those are good men and friends of mine and honest men, but they are uneducated men and they are working all the day and part of the night, principally attending to somebody else's business because they do not understand the first principle of command."

Major Allen Gullion, the Army's new prosecutor in the

case, sharply called off a list of the highest-ranking Navy officers, including Admiral Eberle, the Chief of Naval Operations. "Do you consider that they are hidebound uneducated men?"

"I certainly do."

Sims said he did not agree with Mitchell's idea of a separate air force, but that the Navy was making little or no effective use of air power, and that the country's future was in danger as a result.

A day or so later, when the last of the defense witnesses had come and gone, each one giving a glimpse of inefficiency and confusion in the services, and of the widespread hostility toward development of air power, Reid announced that Mitchell himself would take the stand the next week. Newspapers welcomed this as the climax of the trial. One headline said, "CAPITAL'S LONGING FOR A HERO FILLED PERFECTLY BY MITCHELL." The paper reported public demonstrations each time he appeared outside the courtroom and said that he and Mrs. Mitchell were being entertained "as if he were some visiting prince or potentate."

10

"WHY, THESE MEN
ARE MY FRIENDS!"

Mitchell went to the witness stand pale and tense but with an air of supreme confidence. A newspaper described him at this moment: "Head erect, shoulders thrown back, finely chiseled chin aloft, the very embodiment of defiance and the damnation of all traitors."

Reid said that Mitchell was ready for "a full cross-examination by anybody and everybody in the world."

The lawyer asked Mitchell to tell how he had come home from war in 1919 to crusade for air power, and Billy recalled his talks with French, English and German aviators about the future of warfare. He said the experts were unanimous. "A future contest between nations would be preceded by two things—intensive action of submarines across the seas, and air attack on the nerve centers of the hostile states so as to eliminate the will to fight. . . . The future war would see an elimination probably of the cannon fodder system as it has been practiced for the last two or three hundred years."

Later, Reid had Mitchell list recommendations he had made, almost all of them rejected by the high command:

In 1918, that the Army and Navy combine their supply systems and research.

That overseas air forces be kept at war strength.

That carriers be built, with a capacity of one hundred planes each.

That helium be used in new dirigibles for greater safety, and that they carry aerial torpedoes. Reid asked him to explain this weapon. "It's an American invention," Mitchell said, "a radio-controlled plane that can hit targets from a long distance. Every nation is working hard on that." He also described a "gliding bomb" that could be fired from planes to strike cities many miles away, and said that New York, Washington and other American centers should have aerial defenses, radio, fighter planes, bomb shelters, civilian defense plans. "You might say we have never been able to get a study made of a thing like that in this country." The judges who had fought in the mud trenches of France only seven years before stared blankly at him.

Mitchell went on with an almost endless list of proposals he had made in vain:

Four-engine bombers of 1500-mile range and a ceiling of 30,000 feet, all metal planes, night-flying training, a rank for aviation mechanics, a radio network, machines to load big bombs, inflatable life rafts, United States and hemisphere air routes, air bases in Alaska, variable-pitch propellers for use at varying altitudes, instrument flying. A special need, he said, was a weather reporting service. "Up to about 1920 we were allowed to telephone ahead to find out what the weather was when we were flying, but they cut off those funds, which I think was a very short-sighted thing."

The Army had turned down his pleas for amphibious planes for rescue work, landing gear of skis and skids; for years his pilots were forced to pour gas into their planes from five-gallon cans, and then to pump the fuel by hand, before he could persuade authorities to provide powered pumps.

He had urged building new planes for the annual speed races to spur better design; a new policy of Pacific defense; revised war plans, so that a single commander would direct all arms in the first phase of defense against an air attack. He had been unable to provide self-starters for his planes. "The present method of starting is very inefficient and very dangerous. The men have to pull the propellers and if for any reason there is a backfire, or if the engine fires prematurely, the men are either killed or maimed."

Under Reid's questioning, Mitchell told of the first cross-country flights which had led to development of commercial air routes; of his own flying—more than 200,000 miles in four years; of his Pacific inspection tour, and the speed record he had set in a fighter plane.

After an hour and a half, when he had run out of questions, Reid had Mitchell call out the names of World War battles in which he had fought, more than a dozen of them, and turned him over to Major Gullion for cross-examination by the prosecution.

The crowd laughed at Gullion's first question. "Colonel Mitchell, have you any idea of the estimated wealth of the United States?"

"No."

Gullion said that it was more than $300 billion, and then, in a long series of questions, attempted to show that Mitchell's forecasts of an air-sea war with Japan were absurd—since Japan would need 2500 submarines, by Gullion's estimate, and that these would cost more than the total wealth of the United States. Mitchell only smiled. "I would like to have my own plans financed on such a basis," he said.

Gullion scorned Mitchell's estimate of Japan's ability to wage war. "What is the source of your information?"

"The studies I have made practically all over the northern hemisphere and in Japan, and looking forward into the future so as to render an adequate national defense to this country. That's it."

Gullion used sarcasm in attempts to anger Mitchell. "Now, in your statement of September 5—this factless statement—"

"I object," Reid said.

"You want to stop that Mr. Judge Advocate," the court law officer said.

"I withdraw that," Gullion said, "and I'm very sorry." He turned back to Mitchell with a question about his criticism of recent maneuvers in Hawaii, which Mitchell had not witnessed.

"If you were not aware of the training motives in these exercises, how do you justify your statement?"

"From what I saw in the newspapers."

"Is that your usual source of information?"

"Usually, in respect to the Navy, because I can't get any statements from the Navy."

Gullion said that more planes had been used in the Hawaiian maneuvers than in the Chesapeake bombing tests against old battleships in 1921.

"Yes," Mitchell said, "and they were much more worthless than those we had at Langley Field in 1921."

"The numbers were greater."

"Numbers mean nothing in the air. It is excellence, excellence in materiel and personnel."

Gullion quizzed Mitchell about his criticism of the Navy's Hawaiian flight. "Do you still regard the PN-9 as a really good-for-nothing big, lumbering flying boat?"

"For the purpose of flying from the Pacific coast to Honolulu, I do. I was perfectly certain the ship could not make the trip."

"Do you offer yourself, speaking from San Antonio on September 5, as a better critic of that flight than Commander Rodgers, who . . . commanded the PN-9?"

"I do."

Mitchell insisted that the Navy's pilots for the trip were poorly trained and had inferior equipment, including a radio that would not transmit when the plane went down into the sea.

Gullion read a sentence from Mitchell's statement which accused the Army and Navy of "almost treasonable" handling of national defense, and then asked, "Well, what is treason?"

"There are two definitions of treason," Mitchell said. "One is levying war against the United States or giving aid and comfort to its enemies. The other is to give up or betray . . . perfidy or breach of faith. I believe that the departments, the system, is almost treasonable in that it does not give a proper place to air power in organizing the defenses of the country, which is vital as an element. That is what I believe."

Gullion attacked Mitchell's criticism of the Navy's only carrier, a converted collier, the *Langley*. "Do you know how the *Langley* ranks in size as compared with the carriers existing in the world?"

"I can give you all that data from looking at it. She is useless as a carrier."

"You can't give us an approximate idea?"

"No. Except that she is almost useless as a carrier." (The Japanese were to sink the *Langley* with ease early in World War II.)

"That is an opinion, is it?"

"That is a fact."

"Then you have found a fact. All right."

Reid objected to this baiting of the witness and asked that Gullion's remark be stricken from the record.

Gullion tried to show that Mitchell advocated a new and terrible form of war. "You stated this morning that the soldier in war will no longer be cannon fodder. Will bombing attacks on women and children in another war be more humane simply because they are destroyed in that way instead of by cannon?"

"I can't answer that question."

Gullion paused to complain about the witness to the generals on the bench. "I don't like to make the objection," he said, "but most of my questions are 'yes' or 'no' questions, and I don't think the accused should be permitted to get the signal from his counsel."

Mitchell sprang halfway out of his chair and shook a finger angrily under Gullion's nose. Reid jumped to his feet. "You're liable to encounter considerable trouble if you make that accusation. I want to object to any statement of that kind. I have made no signals to the witness and do not intend to and do not have to. I merely want him to keep within the rules."

At the end of a day of this grilling, the New York *World* reported, Mitchell was "extremely nervous, his eyes sunken, his jaw twitching, often sitting with his head down, "yet every now and then his old-time defiance would flash forth."

The largest crowd of the trial jammed the courtroom the next day, and guards used ropes to control spectators. Many Congressmen and government officials had come, and there was pushing and shoving in the room all day. Gullion and Mitchell responded with lively exchanges.

Gullion read a few lines from Mitchell's book, *Winged Defense* and then showed the court a secret document, a lecture delivered at the General Staff College by Captain Thomas Hart of the Navy.

"What are you trying to do?" Reid asked.

"I'm going to show that the accused cribbed page after page of this book from which he is making money."

"Oh, that's it!"

"Yes."

The crowd hissed Gullion.

"That's fine," Reid said coldly, "and material to the issue in this case—and shows how much you know what this case is about."

"Colonel Mitchell," Gullion said, "did you write all the other pages of this book?"

"That book is under my signature."

"Did you give credit to your sources by footnotes?"

Reid objected. "I don't think it's proper evidence. I'm willing to have the court read it."

"And let the court pay $2.50 each for it?"

The crowd hissed again.

General Howze broke in, "Gentlemen, confine yourselves to the issue in the case."

The prosecutor turned to Mitchell's charge that "the

airmen themselves are bluffed and bulldozed so that they dare not tell the truth," and asked "what officers did you have in mind?"

"I refer to myself principally."

"You dare not tell the truth?"

"Not that I dare not tell the truth, but that I am bluffed and bulldozed."

"You speak in the plural—'the airmen themselves.'"

"Yes."

Gullion sneered. "Do you consider yourself in the plural habitually?"

Reid objected and Gullion read more of Mitchell's charges. "Do you feel that you were sent to 'an out-of-the-way place?'"

"I certainly was."

"Do you consider San Antonio a most out-of-the-way place to which an officer can be sent?"

"It certainly is so far as influencing Air Service development is concerned."

"How about as far as publicity is concerned?"

"That's a question."

Gullion challenged Mitchell's figure on air fatalities and said that it was "twice as safe to fly" in the United States service as in the British.

"Let us see your proof," Reid said.

"The figures are confidential, and I can't show them to you unless the courtroom is cleared," Gullion said.

The court law officer said, "Show them to him." Reid grinned. "Just slip them to me. Will you just whisper them to me?"

Gullion was not amused. He continued to read, saying that United States aviation had only half the deaths suffered by the French, and a fourth of the Italian losses.

"The figures are meaningless," Mitchell said.

"Is your personal observation a safer guide than the statistics actually gathered and published?"

"Yes, sir. Because the statistics don't show that our fliers are restricted to air fields and never get away from them and never take the risks of cross-country runs. You can twist statistics. . . ."

The exchange went on for hours. Gullion finally asked Mitchell about his charge that the Army supported "a propaganda service," and then said, "Did you ever give any information to the press, while Assistant Chief of the Air Service?"

"Often. There was no other way of getting the truth out, I found."

Gullion tried to have the answer stricken from the record, but the court refused. Unexpectedly, Gullion said, "We are through with the witness."

Outside the courtroom, Mrs. Mitchell said she was worried, and Billy tried to cheer her. "Suppose they do find me guilty. Guilty of what? I've committed no crime. Suppose I am dismissed. Well, I've always wanted to hunt big game in Africa. Disgrace? What's the disgrace?"

Many more witnesses appeared in the last stages of the trial. Representative Fiorello La Guardia, the future mayor of New York, a World War pilot, came to help Mitchell, and told reporters, "Why he's not being tried by his peers, but by dogrobbers of the General Staff." Newspaper extras headlined his attack, and when La Guardia took the witness stand later, the judges glared at him. He told of the ineffectiveness of anti-aircraft fire during the war, but Gullion interrupted, "Mr. La Guardia, the newspapers quoted you as saying, 'Billy Mitchell isn't being tried by a jury of his peers, but by nine beribboned dogrobbers of the General Staff.' Were you correctly quoted?"

"I didn't say beribboned."

Laughter halted the court for several minutes. General Howze then said frostily, "The court would like to have you explain what was meant by your characterization of this court."

"From my experience as a member of Congress and from my contact with the General Staff, I'm convinced that the training, background, experience and attitude of officers of high rank are conducive to carrying out the wishes and desires of the General Staff." After a pause La Guardia added, "I want to say that at that time I didn't know General MacArthur was on this court."

Spectators burst into laughter once more, joined by the judges.

"How high in rank does an officer have to get," Howze asked, "before he comes within your characterization?"

"General, it all depends on whether he wants to stay in the Army. There's no difference in the Army from what it is in real political circles. There's no difference. There is the same desire to carry out the wishes of those who control."

Prosecution witnesses came and went as the Army sought to show that Mitchell's criticism was baseless and unfair. Reid grilled them vigorously in cross-examination, much as if he were in a civilian courtroom, and some of the judges were impatient with him. As Reid pressed one witness with a barrage of questions General King lost his temper and called out, "Damned rot!"

Reid whirled on him. "I object to that. This is not damned rot in your mind or anybody else's, and I object to it."

"I was talking to General ——."

"I know, but I heard it."

"I'm sorry, Mr. Reid," King said.

"This may be a little tedious to you, but I have a mission to perform in cross-examination—and I certainly don't want a member of the court making such a remark."

After the court session Reid told reporters he would not call for a mistrial, though he would have grounds for it in any civilian court. The judges themselves were uneasy about King's outburst, but took no action. The trial continued. Witnesses came and went more rapidly.

Captain Alfred Johnson of the Navy admitted that some naval officer had written on an order for a recruiting film, "The object of this is to combat the effect of General Mitchell's testimony and to belittle the value of airplanes."

Lieutenant Commander T. W. Pennoyer, a carrier expert, who appeared next, often hid behind the claim that much Navy information was secret. He tangled with Reid. "Have we ever been furnished plans of the Japanese ships?" Reid once asked.

"You're encroaching on confidential matter, sir."

"But you use encroachment to protect your answers."

Gullion broke in, "I submit that isn't fair. I never heard more straightforward testimony than this."

"You never did, and that is what hurts you," Reid said.

Gullion demanded that Reid apologize to Pennoyer. "I move that the remark of Mr. Reid be stricken from the record, that the witness had made an attempt to protect himself by pleading confidentially."

"I move that it be framed and sent to the Navy Department," Reid said.

Pennoyer finally gave Reid the answer he sought when

he said that the old *Langley* was not a combat carrier.

"Then the United States has not now, nor has ever had, any aircraft carriers?" Reid said.

"Not an effective carrier designed to operate with the fleet."

"That is all," Reid said.

As the end of the trial neared the prosecution called General Summerall, the deposed president of the court. The stiff, proud officer challenged Mitchell's report on Hawaiian defenses and anti-aircraft fire, and Reid finally asked the question for which the crowd was waiting. "Are you friendly with the accused?"

Summerall sat silently and after a long pause Reid said, "All right, did you make this statement—'From now on, Mitchell and I are enemies,'—after you were challenged as president of this court?"

Summerall denied newspaper reports of his angry reaction and said he did not remember using those words. Reid asked him once more if he had called Mitchell his enemy.

"I do not recall making that statement."

"Are you now friendly with the accused?"

"I am indifferent toward the accused."

Reid asked Summerall what he had written to Mitchell's superior, General Patrick, after Billy had criticized the defenses of Hawaii, but Summerall said that was "secret," even if it had not been marked so when it was written.

When Summerall left the court he told reporters, "Mitchell is one of that damned kind of soldier who's wonderful in war and terrible in peace."

Other hostile witnesses took over. General Hugh Drum, the Assistant Chief of Staff, was loud and positive in his opinions: air planes could fly no higher than 12,500 feet, and would never fly so high that they couldn't be seen with a telescope. A dozen anti-aircraft guns could keep any bombing squadron from its objective. Drum and Reid almost came to blows when the general accused the lawyer of being a World War draft dodger, and Reid finally refused to question Drum further because of his belligerent attitude.

Another witness was Lieutenant Colonel Lesley J. McNair of the General Staff, who had been in Hawaii during Mitchell's inspection. McNair said that Mitchell's report had been tossed aside because "it brought up no essential plan which could be accepted" by the Army—but he added, without explanation, that most of Mitchell's suggestions had been in effect before Billy arrived, anyway.

Major General Hanson Ely, commander of the Army War College, condemned Mitchell for his claims that air power could win wars.

Reid cited a quotation: " 'The potentialities of aircraft attack on a large scale are almost incalculable . . . owing to its crushing moral effect. It may impress public opinion to the point of disarming the government and then become decisive.' Do you believe that?"

"No."

"That was said by Marshal Foch, the French Commander-in-Chief. Was he formerly well informed on military tactics?"

"Yes, but all men have dreams and visions."

Reid quoted another opinion. " 'The development of aircraft indicates that our national defense must be supplemented by, if not dominated by, aviation.' "

Ely said he could not agree with that.

"You think it is absolutely absurd?"

"Yes."

"That is the statement of President Coolidge."

"I don't care what it is."

The court ordered the remarks about Coolidge stricken from the record.

General Patrick then took the stand to deny many of Mitchell's charges, but Reid forced him to concede that the United States was almost helpless in the air: bombers did not practice, because bombs were too expensive—fifty cents per pound; new planes were scarce because they cost $16,000 each, and wartime De Havillands could be remodeled for $1800.

"Has the United States any real air force at this time?"

"Yes."

"What is it?"

"A very small one. We have one pursuit group and one bombardment group in this country . . . and two small attack squadrons." He said there were twenty modern pursuit planes and twenty obsolete bombers.

"How about your attack planes?"

"We have no attack planes, and we are using merely planes of other types."

"Have you any real air policy, military or commercial, in this country?"

"It is very difficult to say whether there is any. . . ."

In short, Mitchell had been right, but Patrick could not approve of his manner of saying it.

On December 17, when the trial had dragged on for seven weeks, General Howze called on the lawyers to sum up their cases. Mitchell surprised the court by refusing to allow Reid to speak. Billy accused the court of failing to rule on whether he had proved he was telling the truth in his criticism of aviation policy. Mitchell then made a brief statement himself:

"My trial before this court-martial is the culmination of the efforts of the General Staff of the Army and the General Board of the Navy to depreciate the value of air power and keep it in an auxiliary position, which absolutely compromises the whole system of national defense.

"These efforts were begun as soon as the sound of the cannon had ceased on the Western Front in 1918. When we sank the battleships in 1921, and proved to the world that air power had revolutionized all schemes of national defense, these efforts were redoubled.

"The truth of every statement I have made has been proved by good and sufficient evidence, not by men who gained their knowledge of aviation by staying on the ground, but by actual fliers. To proceed with the case would serve no useful purpose. I have therefore directed my counsel to entirely close out our part of the proceeding without argument."

The Army's lawyers spoke for hours, attacking Mitchell and his airmen. The fliers had not told the truth, Gullion said, "not from dishonesty, but from temperament and habits of thought." They had been led astray by hopes of advancement and Mitchell's "grandiose schemes." Of Mitchell he said, "Is such a man a safe guide? . . . Is he of the George Washington type, as counsel would have you believe? Is he not rather of the all-too-familiar charlatan and demagogue type, like Aaron Burr?

"He is a good flier, a fair rider, a good shot, flamboyant, self-advertising, wildly imaginative, destructive, never constructive except in wild nonfeasible schemes, and never over-careful as to the ethics of his methods.

"Sirs, we ask the dismissal of the accused for the sake of

the Army whose discipline he has endangered and whose fair name he has attempted to discredit . . . for the sake of those young officers of the Army Air Service whose ideals he has shadowed and whose loyalty he has corrupted. . . . Finally we ask it in the name of the American people, whose fears he has played upon, whose hysteria he has fomented."

The courtroom was silent. The prosecution rested, and the case was over. The judges disappeared to reach their verdict.

In a little over two hours, they returned. A very small crowd waited in the courtroom. General Howze warned the crowd to make no demonstration, told Mitchell to stand, and read in a stern voice:

"The court finds the accused:
"Of Specification One—guilty."
Mrs. Mitchell pressed a hand against her lips.
"Of Specification Two—guilty."
He went through the nine charges, calling after each one, "Guilty."

Howze then said, "The court upon secret written ballot . . . sentences the accused to be suspended from rank, command and duty with the forfeiture of all pay and allowances for five years."

The courtroom was soundless as Howze paused. "The court is thus lenient," he said, "because of the military record of the accused during the world war . . . the court is adjourned."

Mitchell had listened to Howze with a slight crooked smile. When the general ceased, reporters crowded around him, but he said, "No, nothing to say. Nothing now." He turned and looked at the court in hurt and wonder. "Why, those men are my friends!" He noticed that General Mac-Arthur was pale. "MacArthur looks like he's been drawn through a knothole," he said. One reporter thought Mitchell very calm, as if he were sorry that the court had not discharged him from the Army outright. Others did not agree. The New York *World* reporter thought Billy's face was bleak with chagrin and defeat. Mitchell went to the long table and shook hands with all his judges, apparently without embarrassment. Two or three Congressmen came to shake Mitchell's hand and promised to fight for him on Capitol Hill. "This case is mighty far from closed," Mitchell said, "I'll tell you that, but I won't have a thing to say about it until the President passes on this."

"MY VALVES
ARE ALL SHOT"

If Mitchell was despondent he gave no sign of it. He waited quietly for more than a month, saying nothing to newspapermen, while President Coolidge considered the verdict of the court. Frank Reid talked to reporters, however, and was full of fight:

"They may think they have silenced Mitchell, but his ideas will go marching on, and those who crucified him will be the first to put his aviation suggestions into practice. He is a 1925 John Brown."

In angry speeches Congressmen threatened to take revenge on the Army, and wrote bills that would have suspended leading generals and slashed their pay. Representative La Guardia sent up a bill that would reduce the authority of court-martials, and others tried to reverse the court's verdict and restore Mitchell's rank. It was all in vain. The bills did not pass, and within a few weeks Congress turned to other things.

President Coolidge acted at last, upholding the sentence,

but restoring part of Mitchell's pay, about $4800 per year. Coolidge said that the country expected its officers to be obedient, otherwise, "there could be no discipline in the Army and the Navy. . . . Discipline is the whole basis of military training." He said that Mitchell had played upon "the horror-stricken state of mind of the people and violently assailed the War Department and the Navy Department" and that the General's conduct had been inexcusable, whatever his motives.

Mitchell said he could not accept this "modified sentence" and become "an object of government charity." He wrote the Army's Adjutant General, "I hereby tender my resignation as an officer in the United States Army to take effect February 1, 1926." The President accepted at once. Mitchell's long career in uniform was over.

Ex-Secretary of War Weeks, in California on vacation, told reporters, "Mitchell wasn't sufficiently punished by the court. He's nothing but a publicity seeker, an advertiser for personal gain, and he knows as well as I know, that what he says about the airplane situation is false."

The next day, Mitchell issued a farewell statement to the press:

"I have done everything possible for my country. After all these years not one dark spot can be found on my record, and not one act which does not redound to the credit of the United States."

He warned of the dangers of the system which had defeated him. "The military bureaucracy, resisting all innovations, has become such that it is impossible to secure any needed changes in the system . . . this is one of the greatest menaces to our free institutions . . . the bureaucratic party, as it might be called, is more powerful than Democrats or Republicans."

He argued once more for a Department of Defense, and a defense policy "based on the abundance of our raw materials, the excellence of our industries, and the remarkable intelligence of our people."

He announced a continuing crusade:

"From now on I feel I can better serve my country and the flag I love by bringing a realization of the true conditions of our national defense straight to the people than by remaining muzzled in the Army.

"I shall always be on hand in case of war or emergency, or whenever I am needed."

He began a new phase of his campaign at once, in a four-month tour of the country that led him into almost every state, speaking nightly, and often several times a day, attracting large crowds. His message was the necessity for building American air power, military and commercial, the danger of the dead hand of the military past, and the urgency of awakening the nation to world conditions. He showed his audiences films of the Chesapeake bombings, the sinking ships going down in clouds of smoke, with gas and burning phosphorous hanging over the ruin of the old U.S.S. *Alabama*.

He attacked the Army vigorously, comparing the General Staff to a board of directors, "And you know what a board is—long, narrow and wooden. . . . The Army is run according to the book. If you look for something on page 14, column 3, and it isn't there, it cannot be. When a general who has seen an airplane from a dugout in France inspects our aviation, he looks at the kitchen and sees what kind of food the boys are having, sees if the grass is cut the proper length. He inspects the hobnails on ground-men's shoes, and if he looks at the airplane, all he inspects is the paint. . . .

"Thousands of officers stationed in Washington spend their time writing novels to each other. . . . The Navy does not like Alaska. Too many Eskimos. The social advantages are not so good as in Hawaii and San Diego. . . . Our idea of protecting the Panama Canal is to go and sit on it instead of creating airplane bases to prevent an enemy approaching. . . ."

He began his tour in Carnegie Hall in New York, in snowy weather, before a small but enthusiastic crowd, and he went into New England, in large cities and small towns, earning from $500 to $1000 each night for his lectures. In Boston, the Army planted a spy in the audience, a captain who reported on Mitchell to Washington as if he were a foreign enemy. "General Mitchell's appearance on the stage was the occasion of prolonged applause. He wore no decorations, had good stage presence but poor speaking voice and poor enunciation . . . the lecture was delivered in a tone of moderation without recourse to elocution."

Mitchell went through New York State, adding a new appeal—asking the public to support his United Air Force Association to aid the cause of air power. He went to Altoona, Pennsylvania, where a crowd of 75,000 greeted him. In Chicago he was welcomed by the City Council, and the city administration helped to swell his audience. In Detroit he found that the White House had telegraphed business leaders, in an effort to discourage attendance at Mitchell's lecture. A newspaper headlined the story, "YAY, MITCHELL—BUT WHISPER IT." Billy spoke to a half-empty house, and an observer wrote President Coolidge's secretary, "No one of any consequence at all met Mr. Mitchell, nor did anyone of consequence hear his speech."

The general drew huge crowds in Ohio and most of the

midwest. In Dayton, admirers launched a Mitchell For President drive, and in Wisconsin he was urged to come home and run for the Senate. Publishers sought him out, and he contracted to write articles for the Hearst newspapers and for several magazines. In Milwaukee, where a crowd of excited war veterans almost crushed him in a welcome at the railroad station, Mitchell yelled to a reporter, "I'll go on with this tour, a fighting tour, until I run out of breath—at the rate I'm going, about May 1!" He wrote his wife, back home in Virginia, that his manager was adding "absurd costs," and that he was earning too little money. "This stuff is tiresome, going around the country, but I am sure it is the right thing. . . . It is having a far-reaching effect."

At Kelly Field in Texas he was entertained by General Frank McCoy, the first of the court-martial judges he had seen since the trial. His glimpse of life at the base depressed him, and he wrote his wife, "My! Betty, I'm glad we're out of the service. The everlasting humdrum existence that they lead. . . . All the poor air people are perfectly despondent. They haven't a single ship that is really safe to fly. . . . All would get out if they could get suitable positions." In El Paso another of his court-martial judges, General Winans, tried to impede plans for Mitchell's lecture by refusing to lend sponsors an old plane to advertise Billy's coming; he also banned signs on the post.

Mitchell wrote his wife, "The Army and Navy have tried in all ways I think to keep this stuff down, but entirely without success." When he reached California and spoke in San Diego, the fleet left port hurriedly, "so that the officers and men could not come."

In May, 1926, he was back home and settled happily at Boxwood, in Middleburg, Virginia, with his wife and children, Lucy and Billy, Jr. He raised fine hunting horses and dogs, rode and hunted often. The Mitchells went to Russia and Germany in 1927, and when they returned Billy warned that the Russians, using German designers, were building a large air force. The Germans, he said, were evading the peace treaty and raising a large new army. He published seventeen magazine articles that year, but few afterward, and only five appeared in 1930, the year that his last book, *Skyways,* was published. The public seemed to be forgetting Mitchell.

With the election of Franklin D. Roosevelt as President there was new interest in national defense, and there was brief talk of Mitchell heading a new Department of Defense, but that soon faded. There was a fresh outburst of prophetic writing from Mitchell, now dealing largely with the Japanese threat: "Are We Ready for War With Japan?" and "Will Japan Try To Conquer The U.S.?"

The Army was still hostile. Mitchell had been flying occasionally at Wright Field in Dayton as a passenger, and an officer there became so concerned that he called Washington. Billy's successor in the Air Service, General James Fechet, sent an official dispatch—the Army had no objection to Mitchell's local flights as a passenger, but officers were warned against "divulging any confidential information . . . any secret or confidential developments." It was as if Billy were a spy rather than the crusader who had been chiefly responsible for developing most of the aviation secrets.

In 1935 Mitchell's health began to fail. He had nine teeth removed, and had a dangerous heart attack. His old friend Alfred Verville, the plane designer, saw him in a Washington club one day and was shocked by Mitchell's pallor and the dullness of his eyes. Mitchell sank into a chair and sighed, "You know, Verville, the doctors tell me my valves are all shot. I guess my bearings are gone, too. But you know, I've lived three lives, and all I wish is that I could stick around to finish up about three books that I have in mind to write—and I want to be around for the next big show."

"What do you mean, General?

"I mean the real air-power war, the real world war."

Verville asked him where he expected the war to start.

"In the same place that it started last time, in Germany, only this is going to be in everybody's backyard. It's going to be the air-power war, and I'd like to be around to see the color of the faces of those who opposed our military aircraft program when they see the real role air power plays."

Verville never saw him again. A week later his wife took him to a New York hospital, "for a rest," his doctors said. But though heart specialists were called in, and Mitchell was placed under an oxygen tent, he was not on the hospital's critical list. His sister, Harriet, visited him from Milwaukee, and he talked of his future plans for the first time since his illness and joked with her, insisting that she get into the oxygen tent with him. A few days later the tent was removed, and Mitchell seemed to improve. Harriet and his wife sat by his bed while he slept on the cold afternoon of February 19, 1936. He never awakened.

His doctor attributed his death to the complications of influenza and to overwork, the strain of the "three lives" Mitchell had led during his fifty-six full years. He was carried to Milwaukee for burial, with old friends like Eddie Rickenbacker attending the funeral. Among his pallbearers were General Frank McCoy, one of the court-martial judges, and Lieutenant Colonel George Catlett Marshall of the Army, who would become supreme U.S. commander during World War II.

Mitchell had been dead only three years when the German air assault on Poland opened the second World War with the weapons that Billy had so long urged upon the United States. As the war began, America had no dive bombers, no long-range bombers, no fighter squadrons ready for war, and few aircraft carriers. World War II was nearing its end in August, 1944, when President Roosevelt made an inspection tour of the remote, chilly Aleutian Islands, which Mitchell had pointed out as a vital link between Alaska and Asia so long before. Roosevelt wrote in his log on August 3:

"If back in 1940 . . . I had said to the Chiefs of Staff of the Army and the Navy, 'Our next war is going to be in the Aleutians and down in the Southwest Pacific,' they would have all laughed at me. They are the experts at that sort of thing. I am not an expert. I am just an ordinary American. We can see now that Americans were caught unprepared because we were ordinary human beings, following the best advice we had at that time."

It was as if Mitchell had never lived.

In 1957 Mitchell's youngest child, William Jr., asked the Air Force to set aside the court-martial verdict. The plea was based on a section of the United States Military Code permitting the Secretary of a military Department to "correct any military record . . . when he considers it necessary to correct an error or injustice."

The Air Force Board for Correction of Military Records (composed entirely of civilians) recommended that the rightness of Mitchell's cause should be admitted and the verdict of the court set aside. The board urged approval of his son's plea to Secretary of the Air Force James H. Douglas.

The Secretary said:

"The history of recent years has shown that Colonel Mitchell's vision concerning the future of air power was amazingly accurate. He saw clearly the shape of things to come in the field of military aviation, and he forecast with precision the role of air power as it developed in World War II and as we see it today. Our nation is deeply in his debt. . . . Colonel Mitchell's views have been vindicated. But while on active duty and subject to the discipline of the military service, he characterized the administration of the War and Navy Departments as incompetent, criminally negligent and almost treasonable.

"Colonel Mitchell was free to resign his commission and to seek to arouse the public in support of his strong views. . . . He chose instead to remain on active duty while making his charges against his service superiors. In taking this course, he was bound to accept the consequences. . . . I can find no ground for concluding at this time, more than thirty years after the President personally approved Colonel Mitchell's conviction, that the trial should not have taken place, or that the court-martial's finding that Colonel Mitchell was guilty of violating the 96th Article of War had no justification in fact.

"It is tragic that an officer who contributed so much to his country's welfare should have terminated his military career under such circumstances. Today, however, I am confident that his services to his country and his unique foresight as to the place of air power in the defense of our country are fully recognized by his countrymen. No more convincing or appropriate recognition could be given than was bestowed on Colonel Billy Mitchell on August 8, 1946, when the President signed a law posthumously bestowing upon him a Medal of Honor 'in recognition of his outstanding pioneer service and foresight in the field of American military aviation.'

"The application is denied."

INDEX

INDEX

ABOUT THE AUTHOR

Burke Davis is a military historian, biographer and novelist who lives in Williamsburg, Virginia, where he is on the staff of the restoration, Colonial Williamsburg. He has written more than twenty books, most of them on military affairs, several of them for younger readers and young adults. Most of these books are still in print, and several have been chosen as among the fifty most notable books of the year by the ALA, and have been placed in the White House library.

Davis spent more than twenty years as a newspaperman, reporter, editorial writer and sports editor, in North Carolina and in Baltimore. He was born in Durham, North Carolina and was educated at Duke University, Guilford College, and the University of North Carolina. His wife, the former Evangeline McLennan, once a foreign correspondent, is managing editor of the nation's oldest newspaper now published, the *Virginia Gazette* of Williamsburg.

With the aid of the Air Force and the Mitchell family,

ABOUT THE AUTHOR

Davis became the first writer to examine the Mitchell court-martial record—forty years after it was locked up by the Army in 1926. He also saw and used previously unknown material in Mitchell's personal military file, one of the most voluminous in Army records. Davis and his wife studied more than 4000 pages of this record on a microfilm reader in their home in recreating the story of the historic trial.

Davis interviewed many old-time fliers and other contemporaries of Mitchell in writing his books about the celebrated aviator and prophet of air power, and much of that research is reflected in his new book.

Burke Davis has also been a lecturer on creative writing at the College of William and Mary.